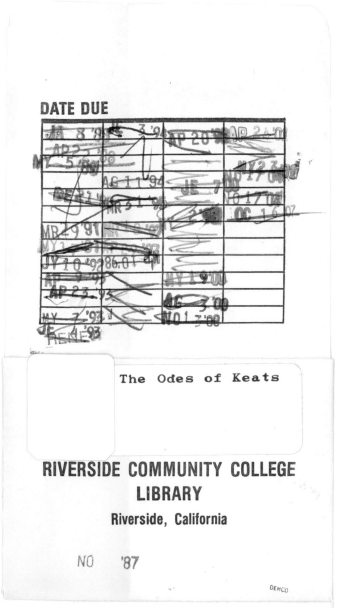

Modern Critical Interpretations
# The Odes of Keats

# Modern Critical Interpretations

*These and other titles in preparation*

*Modern Critical Interpretations*

# The Odes of Keats

*Edited and with an introduction by*

Harold Bloom
*Sterling Professor of the Humanities*
*Yale University*

*Chelsea House Publishers* ◇ 1987
NEW YORK ◇ NEW HAVEN ◇ PHILADELPHIA

© 1987 by Chelsea House Publishers, a division of Chelsea
House Educational Communications, Inc.
  133 Christopher Street, New York, NY 10014
  345 Whitney Avenue, New Haven, CT 06511
  5014 West Chester Pike, Edgemont, PA 19028

Printed and bound in the United States of America

∞ The paper used in this publication meets the minimum
requirements of the American National Standard for
Permanence of Paper for Printed Library Materials,
Z39.48-1984.

Library of Congress Cataloging-in-Publication Data
The Odes of Keats.
  (Modern critical interpretations)
  Bibliography: p.
  Includes index.
  1. Keats, John, 1795–1821—Criticism and
interpretation. 2. Odes—History and criticism. I. Bloom,
Harold. II. Series.
PR4837.K43 1986    821'.7    86-17619
ISBN 0-87754-745-9

# Contents

# Editor's Note

This book gathers together a representative selection of the best criticism available upon the six great odes of John Keats. The essays are reprinted here in the chronological order of their original publication. I am grateful to Hillary Kelleher for her assistance in editing this volume.

My introduction reprints my brief commentaries upon each of the six odes from *The Visionary Company* (1961). It is followed here by Walter Jackson Bate's reading of the "Ode on Melancholy," in which Bate finds another instance of Keats's "vivid acceptance of natural processes." The "fierce dispute" between this heroic naturalism and a consciousness beyond natural entropy is argued again by Morris Dickstein in his study of the "Ode to a Nightingale."

My own revisionary reading of the "Ode to Psyche" as a hymn of poetic belatedness comes fifteen years after my reading of the same poem in the introduction, and testifies to the shadow cast by the conceptual metaphor of "the anxiety of influence." Geoffrey H. Hartman's full-scale study of "To Autumn" is an answer, out of the depths, to that shadow, and seeks to station the poem in that Hegelian womb where images of the divine are somehow reborn.

In a Freudian and Kenneth Burkean analysis of Keats's version of the Sublime mode, Stuart A. Ende reads the "Ode to a Nightingale" as a parable of psychic identification or introjection, in which, as in Freud, the shadow of the object falls upon the ego. Leslie Brisman, reading the "Ode on Melancholy" very differently from W. J. Bate, relates the poem to an exquisite sonnet in Spenser's *Amoretti,* and finds in Keatsian Melancholy the muse of a more difficult (if still fortunate) belatedness, than was invoked in the "Ode to Psyche."

A subtle exegesis of the "Ode on a Grecian Urn" by Paul H. Fry ends in the conclusion that death is the origin or mother of beauty for Keats, a conclusion deeply consonant with the American poetic tradition of Walt

Whitman, Wallace Stevens, and John Ashbery. Helen Vendler masterfully reads the rather neglected "Ode on Indolence" as an unresolved dispute between the deathly and the vital.

This book ends with Martin Aske's analyses of the "Ode to Psyche" and the "Ode on a Grecian Urn" as ambivalent supreme fictions that address themselves to the sorrows of poetic belatedness, without either yielding to those sorrows or seeking wholly to evade them.

# Introduction

## "Ode to Psyche"

The "Ode to Psyche" has little to do with the accepted myth of Eros and Psyche. That myth is itself scarcely classical; it comes very late, and as an obvious and deliberate allegory. Aphrodite, jealous of the beautiful Psyche who is drawing her admirers away, commands Eros to afflict her with love for a base creature. But he falls in love with her, and comes to her regularly, always in the darkness. When, against his wishes, she lights a candle to see him, he flees from her. She quests for Eros by performing tasks set by Aphrodite, the last of which is a descent into the underworld. Psyche's inquiring spirit, which has previously caused her the loss of her lover, now all but destroys her. Warned by Persephone not to open a box sent by that goddess to Aphrodite, Psyche forsakes control again, and is about to be pulled down forever into the darkness when Eros intervenes, persuades Zeus to make Psyche immortal and to reconcile Aphrodite to her. Restored to each other, the lovers dwell together in Olympus.

Keats begins by bringing the reunited Eros and Psyche down to earth. We do not know whether Keats has seen the lovers in a dream or "with awaken'd eyes" in a vision of reality, but either way he has seen them. He finds them at that moment of Keatsian intensity when they are neither apart nor joined together, but rather in an embrace scarcely ended and another about to commence. Eros he recognizes immediately, but Psyche is revealed to him in a moment of astonished apprehension.

The next two stanzas are parallel in structure, and are deliberately contrary to each other in emphasis and meaning. In the first the machinery of worship —altar, choir, voice, lute, pipe, incense, shrine, grove, oracle, and "heat of pale-mouth'd prophet dreaming"—is subtly deprecated. In the second, though the wording is almost identical, the same apparatus is humanized and eulogized. Keats said ironically that he was "more orthodox"

1

in the old Olympian religion than the ancients, too orthodox "to let a heathen Goddess be so neglected." This heathen Goddess is the human-soul-in-love, which can well dispense with the outward worship ironically regretted in the second stanza, but which deserves and needs the inner worship of the imagination that is offered to it in the third stanza.

The changes of wording between the stanzas are so slight that a careless reading may overlook them. In the first, the Olympian hierarchy is "faded," and Psyche is the loveliest of the gods still evident. The other surviving Olympians are Phoebe and Aphrodite, and they live only in the light of the moon and the evening star. They were worshiped by the ancients; Psyche was not, but she is now fairer than either of them:

> though temple thou hast none,
> Nor altar heap'd with flowers;
> Nor virgin-choir to make delicious moan
> Upon the midnight hours;
> No voice, no lute, no pipe, no incense sweet
> From chain-swung censer teeming;
> No shrine, no grove, no oracle, no heat
> Of pale-mouth'd prophet dreaming.

As the catalog piles up, it is deliberately made to seem a little ludicrous, and the thrust (in context) is against the outer ceremonial of organized religion itself, not just against the Olympian worship. The choir is of virgins, and they make "delicious moan" at midnight: a sly hint of the sexual sublimation in aspects of worship. Then comes the long list of negative properties, whose absence makes them seem faintly ridiculous, until at the incantatory climax the celebrant prophet is evoked, with his heat of possession, his "pale-mouth'd" dreaming, as he longs for Phoebe or Aphrodite. The element of sexual suppression is again subtly conveyed.

When Keats turns to the positive, he employs similar phrases with a different emphasis. First comes a very forceful transition in which the sanctified elements are replaced by the poet finding his inspiration in his own perception of the elements:

> O brightest! though too late for antique vows,
> Too, too late for the fond believing lyre,
> When holy were the haunted forest boughs,
> Holy the air, the water, and the fire;
> Yet even in these days so far retir'd
> From happy pieties, thy lucent fans,
> Fluttering among the faint Olympians,
> I see, and sing, and by my own eyes inspir'd.

Too late for antique vows, but in good time for the imaginative vow that Keats is about to give. On one level Keats is still voicing an ostensible regret for the days not "so far retir'd / From happy pieties" (happy in contrast to later pieties), when earth and its forest growths and the other elements were all accounted holy. Now they are not, for other pieties and the analytical mind combine to take away their sanctification. Yet even in these days Keats can *see* one movement, one light, fluttering among the faint Olympians, and because he can see her he can sing, inspired by his own eyes. Atoms of perception become intelligences, as Keats once remarked, because they *see*, they know, and therefore they are God. Seeing Psyche, he knows her, and moves to a union with her in which he becomes a god, a movement of incarnation. The poet is born in his own mind as he moves to become a priest of Psyche, and as a priest he participates in a humanistic and naturalistic communion, an act of the imagination which is a kind of natural supernaturalism. In the passage ending the third stanza the change from "no voice" and "no lute" to "thy voice" and "thy lute" utterly transforms the same phrasing employed earlier:

> So let me be thy choir, and make a moan
>     Upon the midnight hours;
> Thy voice, thy lute, thy pipe, thy incense sweet
>     From swinged censer teeming;
> Thy shrine, thy grove, thy oracle, thy heat
>     Of pale-mouth'd prophet dreaming.

The entire paraphernalia of worship is transformed in this internalization. Not only is Keats himself substituted for the deliciously moaning virgin choir, but Keats's poem, the "Ode to Psyche," which he is in the act of composing, becomes the "moan upon the midnight hours." The voice, the lute, and the pipe become emblems of the poem that features them. The sweet incense rises from the poem itself, now identified as a "swinged censer teeming," and identified also with Keats himself. The particular change in wording here is revelatory—from "chain-swung censer" to "swinged censer," with the mechanical element omitted. The shrine becomes the fane that Keats will build in his own mind; the grove, the visionary foliage that will rise there as "branched thoughts." The oracle or prophet will be Keats in his role of the figure of the youth as virile poet, the youth of the poet's paradise in Collins and Coleridge, the questing poet shepherd in a state of innocence. The final transformation comes in a triumph of contextualization, as no word needs to be changed in "thy heat / Of pale-mouth'd prophet dreaming." This is not the frustration felt by the aspirant for Phoebe or Aphrodite, because it is *thy* heat, Psyche's, and so

Keats and Psyche share it. If it is a reciprocal heat, then the "pale-mouth'd prophet" is at least dreaming of reality.

So far Keats has reached a point parallel to Collins's most imaginative moment in "Ode on the Poetical Character," for Keats has identified himself as a prophet of the loving human soul, and is poised before declaring that the paradise for the soul is to be built by the poet's imagination within the poet's own consciousness. In the final stanza Keats goes beyond Collins, with the general influence of Wordsworth determining the extent of that advance:

> Yes, I will be thy priest, and build a fane
>   In some untrodden region of my mind,
> Where branched thoughts, new grown with pleasant pain,
>   Instead of pines shall murmur in the wind.

Collins wrote in the light of Milton; Keats in the more inward-shining light of Wordsworth. In the lines from "The Recluse," prefacing "The Excursion," Keats had read Wordsworth's invocation of a greater Muse than Milton's:

>                       if such
> Descend to earth or dwell in highest heaven!
> For I must tread on shadowy ground.

That "shadowy ground" is the haunt of Keats's "shadowy thought," and its place is "the Mind of Man," which Wordsworth calls "the main region of my song." Wordsworth seeks his "groves Elysian" in a wedding between "the discerning intellect of Man" and "this goodly universe" of nature. Keats, in the last stanza of "To Psyche," finds the goodly universe to be produced within the discerning intellect by the agency of poetry.

The opening lines of this stanza state that Psyche's temple will be built "in some untrodden region" of Keats's mind. The implication is that the process is one of soul-making in an undiscovered country; to build Psyche's temple is to widen consciousness. But an increase in consciousness carries with it the dual capacity for pleasure or for pain. The thoughts that will grow like branches in that heretofore untrodden region will be grown "with pleasant pain"; the oxymoron, Keats's most characteristic rhetorical device, is peculiarly appropriate to any rendition of an earthly or poet's paradise, a Beulah land where, as Blake said, all contrary statements are equally true.

The branched thoughts, in this inner nature, replace pines, and murmur in the wind of inspiration.

Far, far around shall those dark-cluster'd trees
  Fledge the wild-ridged mountains steep by steep;
And there by zephyrs, streams, and birds, and bees,
  The moss-lain Dryads shall be lull'd to sleep.

It takes an effort to recollect that these mountains and other phenomena are all within the mind. The pastoral landscape is completed by the Dryads, who can no longer be lulled to sleep in the external woods now "retir'd from happy pieties" but who find their repose in this mental paradise. Having created a more ideal nature, Keats proceeds to embower within it a sanctuary for Psyche:

And in the midst of this wide quietness
A rosy sanctuary will I dress
With the wreath'd trellis of a working brain,
  With buds, and bells, and stars without a name,
With all the gardener Fancy e'er could feign,
Who breeding flowers, will never breed the same.

The "wide quietness" framed by the "wild-ridged mountains," themselves plumed by the "dark-cluster'd trees," reminds us of the Wordsworthian landscape near Tintern Abbey, where the steep and lofty cliffs impressed thoughts of deeper seclusion on an already secluded scene, and connected the landscape with the quiet of the sky. But whereas Wordsworth's scene is a given outward phenomenon, Keats's is built up within. And so he refers to the function of his working brain within his general consciousness as being that of a "wreath'd trellis," a gardener's support for clinging vines. In Keats's most definitive vision of a poet's paradise, at the opening of *The Fall of Hyperion*, this natural emblem appears again:

                              and by the touch
Of scent, not far from roses. Turning round
I saw an arbour with a drooping roof
Of trellis vines, and bells, and larger blooms,
Like floral censers, swinging light in air.

It is Psyche's rosy sanctuary, but also the arbor where "our Mother Eve" had her last meal in Paradise, a feast of summer fruits. In the "Ode" the sanctuary is dressed not only with buds and bells but with "stars without a name," for here the unrestricted invention of the Fancy is at work. But Paradise was lost, and the Paradise of the poet's fancy has an ambiguous and fragile nature. What follows is the triumph of Keats's "Ode," and the most complex effect in it: the somber but defiant acknowledgment of invention's limits, and the closing declaration of the human love that surmounts even imaginative limitations. Where Collins's "Ode" ends in a grim acknowledgment that the time cannot be imaginatively redeemed, at least not by himself, Keats chooses to end with an image of an open casement, through which the warm Love, Psyche's Eros, shall yet enter.

Keats prepares his poem's rhapsodical climax by coming to a full but open stop after a couplet that rivals any as an epitome of the myth-making faculty:

> With all the gardener Fancy e'er could feign,
> Who breeding flowers, will never breed the same.

Keats, in his use of "feign" in this context, may be recalling the critic Touchstone in *As You Like It*. Audrey says: "I do not know what poetical is. Is it honest in deed and word? Is it a true thing?" Touchstone replies: "No, truly; for the truest poetry is the most feigning." Keats's rich word "feign," with its mingled dignity and ruin, is parallel to the word "artifice" in Yeats's myth of poetic self-recognition in "Sailing to Byzantium." Yeats appeals to the beings who stand in the holy fire of the state Blake called Eden, where the creator and the creation are one. It is a fire that can be walked through; it will not singe a sleeve. Yet it can consume the natural heart away. This is Yeats's prayer to his masters in the fire, who would include Blake and Shelley and Keats: consume away what is sick with desire and yet cannot know itself, for it is fastened to dying, to the contrary to desire. And, having done this, gather me into the *artifice* of eternity. The gardener Fancy only feigns, and when he makes his artifice, breeds his flower, he cannot make or breed the same again, as a natural gardener could. But the orders of reality contend here; the natural gardener breeds only in finite variety, but the abundance of the imagination is endless, and each imaginative breeding is unique.

The poem "Ode to Psyche" is unique, and also central, for its art is a natural growth out of nature, based as it is upon a very particular act of consciousness, which Keats arrests in all its concreteness. Keats's real parallel among the myth-makers is Wallace Stevens, as Collins's is Coleridge, and Blake's is, more or less, Yeats. Keats's Psyche is a sexual goddess who renews consciousness and thus renews the earth, and for Stevens as for Keats the earth is enough. The ode "To Autumn" finds its companion in Wallace Stevens's "Sunday Morning," and "To Psyche" is closely related to some of the "Credences of Summer." Stevens writes of seeing nature as "the very thing and nothing else," and "without evasion by a single metaphor." Keats grows a foliage within his mind so as to have a natural shrine for Psyche which shall be eternal. Stevens says, take the phenomenon of nature and

> Look at it in its essential barrenness
> And say this, this is the centre that I seek.
> Fix it in an eternal foliage
>
> And fill the foliage with arrested peace,
> Joy of such permanence, right ignorance
> Of change still possible. Exile desire
> For what is not. This is the barrenness
> Of the fertile thing that can attain no more.

The gardener Fancy, breeding flowers, will never breed the same, for his feigning gives us that same barrenness, the barrenness of the fertile thing that can attain no more, a fixed perfection that lacks both the flaw and the virtue of green life. This paradox is more overt in the "Ode on a Grecian Urn" and in "Byzantium," where the glory of changeless metal can scorn common bird or petal, and yet must be embittered by the changing and sexually governing moon. What unites Keats and Stevens is a temper of naturalistic acceptance, without bitterness or protest, of the paradox of the Romantic Imagination. Keats carries the honesty of acceptance to the point where it is impossible to judge whether the flaw or virtue of the gardener Fancy is offered to Psyche as the poet's best gift. "*With all* the gardener Fancy e'er could feign," he says. The final offer is Keats's human absolute; he does not offer Psyche the truth of the Imagination, for he is uncertain of the kind of truth involved, but gives her instead the holiness of the heart's affections:

> And there shall be for thee all soft delight
> That shadowy thought can win,
> A bright torch, and a casement ope at night,
> To let the warm Love in!

There is a play, in these final lines, upon the familiar myth of Eros and Psyche which Keats has put aside in the main body of his ode. The mythical love of Eros and Psyche was an act in darkness; the bright torch burns in the natural tower of consciousness which Keats has built for the lovers' shrine. The open casement may remind us of the magic casements that open on the faery vision of the "Nightingale" ode, in the fading of the song of that more ambitious poem. Here, in "To Psyche," it emphasizes the openness of the imagination toward the heart's affections. The subtle genius of Keats shades his ode even at its exultant surrender; there shall be for the soul "all soft delight / That *shadowy* thought can win." Thought is foliage here, and the green shade will shelter the soul, but the green thought itself is shadowy, which again suggests its limitations. Like the other great Romantics, Keats distrusted the Beulah of earthly repose, the natural garden of a world that he longed for. And, like his major contemporaries, he went on from it to a myth that promised a humanism that could transcend nature's illusions.

## "Ode to a Nightingale"

The "Ode to a Nightingale" opens with the hammer beats of three heavily accented syllables—"My heart aches"— signaling the sudden advent of a state of consciousness unlike the Beulah state of "indolence," soft, relaxed, and feminine, which marks Keats's usual mode of heightened awareness and creativity. Like Shelley in the "Skylark," Keats is listening to an unseen bird whose location he cannot specify—it is "In *some* melodious plot / Of beechen green, and shadows numberless." But the sharp immediacy of its song in nevertheless emphasized, for it sings "of summer in full-throated ease." The effect of the song on Keats is dual and strongly physical, indeed almost deathly, His heart aches, and his sense is pained with a drowsy numbness that suggests, first, having been poisoned; next, having taken a narcotic. Not the sound alone of the song, but Keats's empathizing with the bird, has done this. He is not envious of the bird, but is "too happy" in its happiness. He cannot sustain his own "negative capability" in this case; he has yielded his being too readily to that of the bird.

And yet, he welcomes this dangerous vertigo, for the next stanza of the poem seeks to prolong his condition by its wish for drunkenness, for "a beaker full of the warm South." The slackening intensity from poison to narcotic to wine is itself a return to an ordinary wakeful consciousness, a sense of the usual reality from which Keats here would "fade away into the forest dim," to join the nightingale in its invisibility and enclosed joy; to leave behind the world of mutability, where every increase in consciousness is an increase in sorrow. But the leave-taking is the contrary of Keats's expectation; the flight is not an evasion, but an elaboration of waking reality:

> Away! away! for I will fly to thee,
> > Not charioted by Bacchus and his pards,
> But on the viewless wings of Poesy,
> > Though the dull brain perplexes and retards:
> Already with thee!

Suddenly, having put aside the last aid to invocation, but by the act of writing his poem, he is where he wills to be, with the nightingale. The wings of Poesy are "viewless," not just because they are invisible, but because the flight is too high for a vision of the earth to be possible. And the state that now commences is a puzzle to the retarding "dull brain." The sweep of the imagination here is more than rational in its energy. Between the ecstatic cry of "Already with thee!" and the bell-like tolling of the word "forlorn" at the poem's climax, Keats enters the inner world of his poem, that highest state of the imagination which Blake called Eden. The mystery of Keats's unresolved contraries is in his quite anti-Blakean association of this state of more abundant life with what seems to be the death impulse. What for Blake is a state of greater *vision* is for Keats the realm of the *viewless*:

> Already with thee! tender is the night,
>   And haply the Queen-Moon is on her throne,
>     Cluster'd around by all her starry Fays;
>       But here there is no light,
> Save what from heaven is with the breezes blown
>   Through verdurous glooms and winding mossy ways.

It is the night that is tender, the paradoxical darkness of the Keatsian vision constituting the mark of that tenderness. Nature is not blacked out; moon and stars may be present, but their light must first submit to the diminishing maze through which the night winds are blown.

Sight goes; the other senses abide in this trance, which at once equals nature and poetry. He cannot see, but odor, taste, and sound, in an instructive ordering, are called upon to describe the phenomena of the world he has at once entered and created. First, odor and taste, in the form of "soft incense" and "dewy wine":

> I cannot see what flowers are at my feet,
>   Nor what soft incense hangs upon the boughs,
> But, in embalmed darkness, guess each sweet
>   Wherewith the seasonable month endows
> The grass, the thicket, and the fruit-tree wild;
>   White hawthorn, and the pastoral eglantine:
>     Fast fading violets cover'd up in leaves;
>       And mid-May's eldest child,
> The coming musk-rose, full of dewy wine,
>   The murmurous haunt of flies on summer eves.

The sensuous imagery here is the luxury of the lower paradise, of the Gardens of Adonis or of Beulah, but set in a context more severe. The odors and tastes are almost those of a more abandoned Milton, a blind poet intensifying the glory he cannot apprehend. But this is closer to the blindness of faith, the evidence of things not seen. Keats cannot see the flowers, but they do him homage at his feet. The "soft incense hangs upon the boughs" for him; and the darkness is "embalmed," a hint of the death wish in the next stanza. The month has kept faith; it is seasonable, and so aids Keats in guessing the identity of each odor. The significance of the "musk-rose" is that it is "coming," still a potential, for it is "mid-May's eldest child" and Keats is writing his ode early in May. Even as he anticipates the taste of the "musk-rose, full of dewy wine," Keats empathizes in advance with the insects, tasting of that wine on still-to-come summer eves. The rose as "*murmurous* haunt of flies" summons in the sense of hearing:

> Darkling I listen; and, for many a time
> I have been half in love with easeful Death,
> Call'd him soft names in many a mused rhyme,
> To take into the air my quiet breath.

He listens, in the nightingale's own darkness, to the ecstasy of the bird's song. A clue to the poet's deliberate blinding of himself is heard here in a slight but haunting echo of a plangent passage of Milton. In the great invocation to light which opens book 3 of *Paradise Lost*, the blind poet prepares himself to describe the glory of God the Father, "bright effluence of bright essence increate," a light so intense as to put out our earthly sight. As he reflects on his own sightless eyes, Milton's thoughts turn to the nightingale singing in darkness:

> Then feed on thoughts, that voluntary move
> Harmonious numbers; as the wakeful Bird
> Sings darkling, and in shadiest Covert hid
> Tunes her nocturnal note.

How consciously Keats remembered this passage one cannot say, but it contains the whole kernel of "Ode to a Nightingale," including the identification of poet and bird in their situations; involuntary in Milton, voluntary in Keats.

As he listens in the bird's own darkness, Keats approaches that supreme act of the Romantic Imagination so prevalent in his master, Wordsworth, the fluid dissolve or fade-out in which the limitations of time and space flee

away, and the border between being and nonbeing, life and death, seems
to crumble:

> Now more than ever seems it rich to die,
>   To cease upon the midnight with no pain,
>     While thou art pouring forth thy soul abroad
>       In such an ecstasy!
>   Still wouldst thou sing, and I have ears in vain—
>     To thy high requiem become a sod.

Two attitudes toward death, the first shading into the second, are
involved in this beautiful but disturbed stanza. Previous to the occasion
this ode celebrates, the poet says, he has frequently invoked Death, under
his "soft names" of ease, calling on Death to take his breathing spirit "into
the air," that is, to die by the very act of exhaling. As he has called upon
Death in "many a mused rhyme," this exhaling is equivalent to the act of
uttering and composing his poem, and we are reminded that spirit means
both soul and breath, and that the poet invoking his muse calls upon a
breath greater than his own to inspirit him. Death, then, is here a muse,
but this was previously only partly the case:

> I have been *half* in love with easeful Death.

But

> Now more than ever seems it rich to die,
>   To cease upon the midnight with no pain.

"Rich" and "cease" are marvelously precise words. Now, in the shared
communion of the darkness out of which the nightingale's song emerges,
it seems rich to die, and he is *more than half* in love with easeful Death. For
he has reached the height of living experience, and any descent out of this
state into the poverty of ordinary consciousness seems a death-in-life, a
pain to be avoided, in contrast to the life-in-death "with no pain" to be
maintained were he "to cease upon the midnight." "To cease," suddenly
not to be, and thus to cross over into nonbeing attended by the "requiem,"
the high mass of the nightingale's song. For the nightingale itself is pouring
forth its soul abroad in an ecstasy that transcends the division between life
and death; the bird lives, but its breath-soul is taken into the air as it gives
itself freely in the extension of its ecstasy.

Two notes deliberately jar with this passion: "and I have ears in vain—"
and "become a sod." At the very moment of Keats's most exultant self-

surrender to the bird's song, he yet intimates his own mortality, his separateness from the immortality of the song:

> Thou wast not born for death, immortal Bird!
>   No hungry generations tread thee down;
> The voice I hear this passing night was heard
>   In ancient days by emperor and clown:
> Perhaps the self-same song that found a path
>   Through the sad heart of Ruth, when, sick for home,
>     She stood in tears amid the alien corn;
>       The same that oft-times hath
>   Charm'd magic casements, opening on the foam
>   Of perilous seas, in faery lands forlorn.

The sadness of this stanza is double, for there is the explicit burden of
Keats as he explores his separateness from the bird's song, and the implicit
lament in the stanza's coming to rest upon the fateful word "forlorn," the
repetition of which serves to shatter the inner world of the nightingale's
song. The pathos of the reference to Ruth becomes tragic in its implied
transference to the poet, through whose heart the self-same song now finds
its path to indicate *his* coming alienation, not from home, but from the
song itself. The closing lines of the stanza, with their hint of the Spenserian
world, to Keats the universe of poetry itself, are a final presage of the loss
that is to come. The "faery lands" are forlorn, not that the poet has forsaken
them, but that, like the bird's song, they have abandoned him:

> Forlorn! the very word is like a bell
>   To toll me back from thee to my sole self!
> Adieu! the fancy cannot cheat so well
>   As she is fam'd to do, deceiving elf.
> Adieu! adieu! thy plaintive anthem fades
>   Past the near meadows, over the still stream,
>     Up the hill-side; and now 'tis buried deep
>       In the next valley-glades:
>   Was it a vision, or a waking dream?
>   Fled is that music:—Do I wake or sleep?

The double tolling of "forlorn" converts the nightingales's song into
a "plaintive anthem," a requiem for the shattered communion between poet
and song, as it rings the poet back to the isolation of his sole self. The
movement of imagination becomes the deception of an elf, like the Belle
Dame, Keats's triple mistress, Poetry, Consumption, and Death. The song

fades with the unseen flight of the bird, until it is "buried deep." There remains only the resolution of the nature of the poetic trance—fully manifest, as in a vision, or merely the latent content of a waking dream? The answer is uncertain, for "fled is that music." At the close, Keats is left pondering the contraries: are the act and state of creation a heightening or merely an evasion of the state of experience? Once back in experience, the honest answer is only in the continued question, both as to fact and to will: "Do I wake or sleep?"

## "ODE ON MELANCHOLY"

The difficulties of the "Ode on Melancholy" are infrequently realized because the poem is not often closely read. Yet even a superficial reading involves us in Keats's deliberately unresolved contraries. The admonition of the first stanza is against false melancholy, courted for the sake of the supposed oblivion it brings. But oblivion is not to be hired; for Keats true melancholy involves a sudden increase in consciousness, not a gradual evasion of its claims.

Keats canceled the initial opening stanza of this ode presumably because he saw that the poem's harmony was threatened if fully half of it was concerned with the useless quest after "the Melancholy." His sense of proportion did not fail him in this, and yet something went out of the poem with the exclusion of that stanza:

> Though you should build a bark of dead men's bones,
>     And rear a phantom gibbet for a mast,
> Stitch shrouds together for a sail, with groans
>     To fill it out, blood-stained and aghast;
> Although your rudder be a dragon's tail
>     Long sever'd, yet still hard with agony,
>         Your cordage large uprootings from the skull
>     Of bald Medusa, certes you would fail
>         To find the Melancholy—whether she
>         Dreameth in any isle of Lethe dull.

The "whether" in the ninth line may be read as "even if." This remarkable and grisly stanza is more than the reverse of an invitation to the voyage. Its irony is palpable; its humor is in the enormous labor of Gothicizing despair which is necessarily in vain, for the mythic beast, Melancholy, cannot thus be confronted. The tone of the stanza changes with the dash in line 9; with it the voice speaking the poem ceases to be ironical.

With the next stanza, the first of the received text, the voice is passionate, though its message is the same. By excluding the original first stanza, Keats lost a grim humor that finds only a thin echo at the poem's close. That humor, in juxtaposition to the poem's intensities, would have been parallel to successful clowning in a tragedy.

As the poem stands, the idle quest after the Melancholy is yet inviting:

> No, no, go not to Lethe, neither twist
>   Wolf's-bane, tight-rooted, for its poisonous wine;
> Nor suffer thy pale forehead to be kiss'd
>   By nightshade, ruby grape of Proserpine;
> Make not your rosary of yew-berries,
>   Nor let the beetle, nor the death-moth be
>     Your mournful Psyche, nor the downy owl
> A partner in your sorrow's mysteries;
>   For shade to shade will come too drowsily,
>   And drown the wakeful anguish of the soul.

What is most important here is "*too* drowsily" and "*wakeful* anguish." The truest parallel is in the first stanza of the "Ode to a Nightingale." There the drowsiness is not excessive, it numbs, but the soul's anguish remains wakeful. The properties of questing after the Melancholy are there also: hemlock, a dull opiate, Lethe, but only in the form of "as though." The melancholy is genuine there, as it is here. It is as though Keats had quested after the epiphanies of these poems, but he has not. The negative grace of the state of being these odes embody falls suddenly, comes with the sharp immediacy of a blow. "My heart aches"; the three heavily accented syllables begin the poem by battering three times at the poet's and our consciousness. "But when the melancholy fit shall fall / Sudden from heaven . . ." is the equivalent in this ode. But when it falls without one's having provoked it, "Then glut thy sorrow"; one need show no restraint in feeding it further. On what? The melancholy fit has fallen as the rains of April fall, to "foster the droop-headed flowers," to cover the hills with green. The shock is that this green fostering, for all its beauty, *is* like the fall of melancholy, for April's green is here called "an April shroud." The enduring color of fresh life is only a grave color, and so your sorrow can also be glutted on the loveliness of such supposedly nonsorrowful emblems as a morning rose, a shore rainbow, or the wealth of globed peonies. To complete the complexity, Keats offers as food for sorrow the *wealth* of one's beloved's "rich anger."

The force of this second stanza is that it is inexplicable, unresolved, until it is suddenly clarified by the first line of the final stanza:

> She dwells with Beauty—Beauty that must die.

The line relies on its immediate expository force after the puzzle of the preceding stanza; it requires a long pause after reading. The emphasis needs to be put upon "*must* die"; the anger of the mistress, which so delights the sadism-hunting scholar, is significant only in its richness, not in any sexual implication. It is rich because it offers a possibility of feeding deeply upon an animated beauty that is doomed to lose all motion, all force. Animation, as in its root meaning, here reveals the living soul in full activity, with the special poignance that in this poem is definitive of true melancholy, consciousness of mutability and death. Like Wallace Stevens in "Sunday Morning," "Esthétique du Mal" (especially section 15, the poem's conclusion), and "The Rock," Keats is insisting on the mingled heroic ethic and humanistic aesthetic that the natural is beautiful and apocalyptic precisely because it is physical and ephemeral. Keats's contrast is in his tense insistence that *something* in nature *must* prevail, and his final despair that nothing can, even as the parallel and contrast to Stevens is Yeats, in his insistence (however ironic) that Byzantine realities are superior to mere natural beauties. Spenser in the *Mutabilitie* Cantos and Milton throughout his work resolve these conflicts by a cosmic dialectic. It remained for Blake and Wordsworth, in their very different ways, to humanize these resolutions. With younger and modern Romantics it has been too late in the day to offer full measure in these conflicts; bitterness, however visionary, necessarily keeps breaking in.

The magnificence of the final stanza of "Ode to Melancholy" is in its exactness of diction as it defines the harmony of continued apprehension of its unresolved contraries. Only Beauty that *must* die is beauty; Joy cannot be present without simultaneously bidding adieu; and *aching* Pleasure (the adjective triumphantly embodies a pair of contraries) is immanent only by turning to poison for us, even as we sip its real (not supposed) honey. For, like the rest of Keats's odes, this poem is tragic; it reaches beyond the disillusionments of a state of experience into the farther innocence of a poet's paradise, as in the shrine of Moneta in the *Fall of Hyperion*, to which this is surely a reference (the "has" helps establish it):

> Ay, in the very temple of delight
> Veil'd Melancholy has her sovran shrine.

And, as in the *Fall of Hyperion*, this truth is seen by none except those who earn the poet's melancholy, which is not to be usurped. The *strenuous* tongue does not simply sip the grape's juice; it *bursts* the grape of Joy, with the inevitable double consequence of tasting might and the sadness of might, Moneta's or the Melancholy's double aspect, the Goddess as Muse and as Destroyer:

> And be among her cloudy trophies hung.

## "ODE ON A GRECIAN URN"

The still urn is a bride of quietness, but the marriage is unconsummated; the urn speaks. By speaking, it reveals itself as only a "foster-child of silence and slow time"; its true parents are its creator and marble, but its creator communicates through silence, and the unchanging marble has arrested time, and slowed it toward the eternity of art.

The urn as sylvan historian expresses a tale more sweetly than our rhyme because it presents a tale in space and without the duration of time. Liberated from the sourness of temporal presentation, the tale lacks the either/or referential clarity of language:

> What leaf-fring'd legend haunts about thy shape
>> Of deities or mortals, or of both,
>>> In Tempe or the dales of Arcady?
>> What men or gods are these? What maidens loth?
> What mad pursuit? What struggle to escape?
>> What pipes and timbrels? What wild ecstasy?

The scene cannot quite be identified, except in its deliberately typical elements. Reluctant maidens flee the mad pursuit of men or gods, but the struggle and reluctance are only part of a myth of pursuit, a ritual of delayed rape spurred on to wild ecstasy by pipes and timbrels. The sexual power of the depicted scene is one with the aesthetic; it depends on potential, on something ever more about to be, and suggests the sense of possible sublimity that art can communicate. In the second stanza, Keats intensifies the expectation:

> Heard melodies are sweet, but those unheard
>> Are sweeter; therefore, ye soft pipes, play on;
> Not to the sensual ear, but, more endear'd,
>> Pipe to the spirit ditties of no tone.

The taking famishes the receiver; it is the greatest of the Romantic paradoxes. The darkness of this situation is presented in "La Belle Dame sans Merci," but here Keats explores the twilight. Shelley thought good and the means of good irreconcilable, and made love and poetry the good. In Keats the means can serve the end of good, but tend to serve it too well. The accomplished good requires the rhetoric of the oxymoron, where every qualifier negates what is qualified. And so fulfillment for Keats is a betrayal of potential. The ideal for Keats is to be poised before experience. The ideal for Shelley is to find an experience in which the means and the end, the subject and the object, become indistinguishable one from the other.

As he gazes at the urn's musicians, Keats asks them to play on tonelessly, piping only to his spirit. A train of association carries from the soundless song through the trees that will never know winter to the sexual stasis of the kiss that cannot take place. The gardener Fancy of the "Ode to Psyche" feigned, but breeding flowers he never bred the same. The happy melodist, unwearied, forever pipes songs that are forever new. The urn's youth is forever panting, but also forever young. All these, the urn's foliage, song and singer, beloved and lover, are

> All breathing human passion far above,
> That leaves a heart high-sorrowful and cloy'd,
> A burning forehead, and a parching tongue.

They can scorn the complexities of blood and mire, the common bird and the human singer, and the lover who moves in flesh. The art of Keats triumphs in the line "All breathing human passion far above," for to Keats nothing is more to be desired than "breathing human passion," the sexual experience, which heightens nature to its own limits. For Keats, as for Wordsworth before him, to call something "human" is to eulogize it. Keats does not deprecate the human in this line or anywhere else, and we miss the line's meaning if we do not read it as including its own contrary. The "more happy, happy love" depicted on the urn is as far below breathing human passion as it is far above. A mouth that has no moisture and no breath may be able to summon breathless mouths, but it can as easily be called death-in-life as life-in-death. Confronted by an impassable paradox, Keats resolves his poem by a dialectic dependent on the simultaneous existence and nonexistence of what is presented by art. In a perfect Shakespearean stanza, he shifts perspective and looks at another picture on the urn:

> Who are these coming to the sacrifice?
> To what green altar, O mysterious priest,
> Lead'st thou that heifer lowing at the skies,
> And all her silken flanks with garlands drest?

What little town by river or sea shore,
  Or mountain-built with peaceful citadel,
    Is emptied of this folk, this pious morn?
And, little town, thy streets for evermore
  Will silent be; and not a soul to tell
    Why thou art desolate, can e'er return.

What Keats sees is a procession; the rest is conjecture. The green altar and the little town exist not on the urn but in the past and future that are phenomenological implications of the poem's existence. They belong to the world that critics of poetry have no reason to inquire into: the world of the childhood of Shakespeare's heroines, and of the married life of Jane Austen's Mr. and Mrs. Collins. This is precisely the world that is not given by a work of art. Keats speculates on it for just that reason, to establish what are the limits of poetry. The nature of poetic time, Keats finds, is such that it teases us out of thought, just as eternity defies our conceptualizations. The procession has emptied some little town, but that town is far in what Shelley called the Unapparent. The procession, because it is portrayed, both is and is not, as Hamlet is and is not. The discursive antithesis between being and nonbeing is revealed by art as a conceptual fiction, a convenience for the tired imagination. The little town is not, even by the canons of art, and the imagination can tell us nothing of it. There is not a soul to tell us why it is desolate, and so the reality of art is only in its eternal present. So also the urn is an eternal present, and its freedom from the restrictions of time eludes our categorization:

O Attic shape! Fair attitude! with brede
  Of marble men and maidens overwrought,
With forest branches and the trodden weed;
  Thou, silent form, dost tease us out of thought
As doth eternity: Cold Pastoral!

Keats begins his final stanza by reminding himself that it is only an artifice of eternity before him. The men and maidens are merely wrought over the urn's surface; they are but marble. Yet the weed is trodden beneath their feet, evidence which teases thought's antitheses. We cannot think of eternity because duration is inextricable with our thinking; time passes as we try to apprehend timelessness. The urn is a silent form, and speaks to us. Its subject is a passionate idyl, and yet it is a cold pastoral, for marble sensuality is at an extreme from "a burning forehead, and a parching tongue." Cold though it be, it is a friend to man, for its temporal freedom intimates to us another dimension of man's freedom:

When old age shall this generation waste,
 Thou shalt remain, in midst of other woe
 Than ours, a friend to man, to whom thou say'st,
 "Beauty is truth, truth beauty,"—that is all
  Ye know on earth, and all ye need to know.

Keats wrote, in one of his letters, that what the imagination seizes as beauty *must* be truth. The imagination he compared to Adam's dream, during which Eve was created. Adam woke to find it true, presumably because she *was* beautiful. The urn's beauty is truth because age cannot waste it; our woes cannot consume it. The urn's truth, its existence out of time, is beauty because such freedom is beautiful to us. The condition of man, for Keats, is such that all we shall ever know we know on earth, and the sum of our knowledge is the identity of beauty and truth, when beauty is defined as what gives joy forever, and truth as what joy seizes upon as beauty. The image of an eddying joy, making its own definitions by circularity, closed Coleridge's "Dejection: An Ode" and reappears in abstract form at the close of Keats's "Ode on a Grecian Urn." To know the truth of the imagination is to live again, and living, the soul will know the beauty of its own truth. The defiant naturalist in Keats takes him a liberating step beyond Coleridge; the soul that knows the identity of beauty and truth knows also its own freedom, which is all it needs to know.

## "ODE ON INDOLENCE"

In the "Ode on Indolence" Keats loafs and invites his soul to consider the lilies of the field. The poem is in the mood of the "Grecian Urn," but the mood is turned inward toward Keats himself. The subject is not poetry, but the poet.

Both odes begin with a confrontation of a classical scene, but in the "Indolence" Keats starts with an allegory, and then compares the personified figures to those on an urn. The strength of his obsessions—Love, Ambition, Poesy—and his rueful disregard for them in favor of what is seen as a more imaginative fourth abstraction, Indolence, determine the shape of a poem remarkable in itself and illustrative of the conflicts within the poet.

The three figures move like three graces, serene and disinterested, but they are Keats's three fates, and their triple passing has an ominous potential for him. They restore him to that state of consciousness he seeks to evade:

Ripe was the drowsy hour;
 The blissful cloud of summer-indolence

> Benumb'd my eyes; my pulse grew less and less;
> Pain had no sting, and pleasure's wreath no flower:
> O, why did ye not melt, and leave my sense
> Unhaunted quite of all but—nothingness?

The poem dismisses Love as that which can neither be defined nor located, and Ambition as mutable, but it makes a more involved farewell to Poesy. She is a "maiden most unmeek," even "my demon," and yet Keats loves her more, the more of blame is heaped upon her. Even she, whose faults are thus translated to virtues, has no joys to give Keats which are

> so sweet as drowsy noons,
> And evenings steep'd in honied indolence.

The sensuous concreteness of indolence makes the three figures ghosts by contrast. Keats's mood is a *penseroso* one; he is sinking back deliberately into the bower celebrated as the poet's first phase in "Sleep and Poetry." Yet he makes it clear that he wants a creative repose, to gather force for his final attempts at poetry:

> Farewell! I yet have visions for the night,
> And for the day faint visions there is store.

He parallels Shelley's lyric "To Night," in which imaginative consciousness is equated with natural darkness, and ordinary consciousness with the heavy burden of noon. The farewell to Poesy in the "Indolence" is a farewell to the conventional idea of poetry, the pseudopastoral namby-pamby land of Leigh Hunt:

> For I would not be dieted with praise,
> A pet-lamb in a sentimental farce!

This is Keats's break with any sentimentalities about nature, and its "places of nestling green for poets made." From his defiant indolence, a true poet's trance, there arises the vision of tragic humanism that ends his career as poet, *The Fall of Hyperion*.

## "TO AUTUMN"

"To Autumn" is the subtlest and most beautiful of all Keats's odes, and as close to perfection as any shorter poem in the English language. That is of course cliché, but it cannot be *demonstrated* too often (it is more frequently asserted than evidenced). The incredible richness of this ode is such that it will sustain many readings, and indeed will demand them. To paraphrase G. Wilson Knight, "To Autumn" is a round solidity casting shadows on the flat surfaces of our criticism; we need as many planes at as many angles as we can get.

The argument of "To Autumn" is largely implicit. The problem here is to externalize it without removing it from the poem's own context.

The Autumn of the first stanza is a process and a beneficent agricultural conspirer, plotting secretly with the sun to bring ripeness to a state of all. The stanza is aureate, Spenserian in the globed fullness of its style, replete with heavily accented, single-syllabled parts of speech. As process Autumn loads, blesses, bends, fills, swells, plumps, and sets budding. The only receptive consciousness of all this activity is that of the bees, who sip their aching pleasure nigh to such a glut that "they think warm days will never cease," for the honey of harvest pleasure has "o'er-brimm'd" their natural storehouses. The fullness of nature's own grace, her free and overwhelming gift of herself, unfallen, is the burden of this ripe stanza. There is only a slight, but vital premonitory shading: the *later* flowers have deceived the bees.

The first stanza is natural process; the remaining two stanzas are sensuous observation of the consequences of that process: first, sights of the harvest in its final stages; then, postharvest sounds, heralding the coming-on of winter. The sequence of the three stanzas then is preharvest ripeness, late-harvest repletion, and postharvest natural music. The allocation of the senses is crucial: the late-harvest art is plastic and graphic—the art of millennium. The art past ripeness and harvest is the art of the ear, apocalyptic, the final harmonies of music and poetry. Here Keats, like Shelley, is Wordsworth's pupil. In the Intimations Ode the visible glory departed with the summer of the body; the ear, far inland, could yet hear the immortal sea, and so brought the eye back to the autumnal coloring of a sobered but deepened imagination. The same process of heightened autumnal vision is celebrated by Shelley in the final stanzas of his "Hymn to Intellectual Beauty" and "Ode to the West Wind." A more serene triumph awaits the modification of Wordsworth's myth in the final stanza of "To Autumn." The very same movement from sight to sound to final sight may be traced also in the Night the Ninth of Blake's *The Four Zoas*, where the beauty of the harvest of Millennium yields to the clamor of Apocalypse, to be succeeded by a final beauty beyond harvest. The ultimate literary archetype for all this Romantic tradition is of course Biblical.

As the second stanza of "To Autumn" opens, we see Autumn already "amid" her store. The promised overabundance of the first stanza has been fulfilled; the harvest plot has been successful, the blessing so overflowing that nature's grace abounds. Autumn is no longer active process, but a female overcome by the fragrance and soft exhaustion of her own labor. She is passive, an embodiment of the earthly paradise, the place of repose, after the sexual and productive activity hinted at by her having been "close bosom-friend of the maturing sun." But she is also the peasant girl drunk with the odors and efforts of gathering, winnowing, reaping, and gleaning. She sits "*careless*" on the granary floor; the word is very rich. She is careless because there is more to be stored, though she sits, and yet amid all the fresh abundance she can indeed be without care. But the wind, softly lifting her hair, which *is* the unreaped grain, reminds us of the winnowing yet to be done. Again, she lies on her "half-reap'd furrow sound asleep, drows'd with the fume of poppies," late bee-deceiving flowers, which in a sense deceive her also. But the poem celebrates her drowsiness even as it gently chides her, for her hook, in *sparing* the next swath, spares also its twined flowers.

The final four lines of the stanza take us to the very end of harvest, the gleaner bearing her laden head so steadily as to suggest motionlessness even as she moves, which further suggests the running-down to stasis of a process. Finally we are shown the girl patiently watching, hours by hours, the meaningful sameness of the "cyder-press" with its final oozings, the last wealth of complete process itself. With those "hours by hours" we are ready for the music of time in the final stanza. We begin with only the "stubble-plains," but even as they are seen to have their own peculiar visual beauty, so we are able to say that the songs of Spring have been replaced by a different but not a lesser music.

> Where are the songs of Spring? Ay, where are they?
> Think not of them, thou hast thy music, too,—
> While barred clouds bloom the soft-dying day,
> And touch the stubble-plains with rosy hue;
> Then in a wailful choir the small gnats mourn
> Among the river sallows, borne aloft
> Or sinking as the light wind lives or dies;
> And full-grown lambs loud bleat from hilly bourn;
> Hedge-crickets sing; and now with treble soft
> The red-breast whistles from a garden croft;
> And gathering swallows twitter in the skies.

This stanza looks back to the concluding lines of Coleridge's "Frost at Midnight," where we hear

> the redbreast sit and sing
> Betwixt the tufts of snow on the bare branch
> Of mossy apple-tree, while the nigh thatch
> Smokes in the sun-thaw

and also forward to the final stanza of Stevens's *Sunday Morning*, where

> at evening,
> In the isolation of the sky,
> Casual flocks of pigeons make
> Ambiguous undulations as they sink
> Downwards to darkness, on extended wings.

Coleridge is extolling the sweetness even of winter as it will present itself to the country-reared, still-infant Hartley. Stevens, possibly remembering Keats even as Keats may be remembering Coleridge, is offering an image of natural death as an imaginative finality, a human consummation to be wished, though not devoutly. Keats is doing both: praising the redbreast and winter's other singers, and finding in the predeparture twitterings of the gathering swallows an emblem of natural completion. Winter descends here as a man might hope to die, with a natural sweetness, a natural movement akin to the extended wings of Stevens's pigeons or the organizing songs of Keats's swallows as they gather together for flight beyond winter. The day dies soft in this great stanza; the late flowers and poppies of stanzas 1 and 2 are replaced by the barred clouds that bloom the twilight and touch the stubble-plains with rosy hue. And though the *small* gnats mourn in a wailful choir, the sound of their mourning is musically varied by the caprice of the *light* wind, as it lives or dies; the poet's touch itself is light here. A final music replaces the lightness of the mourning. The "full-grown lambs" are now ready for their harvest, having completed their cycle. The "hedge-crickets" are heard across the exhausted landscape; the winter singer, the "red-breast," adds his soft treble, and the departing birds, seeking another warmth, close the poem, which has climaxed in an acceptance of process beyond the possibility of grief. The last seven lines are all sound: natural music so varied and intense as to preclude even natural lament. We feel that we might be at the end of tragedy or epic, having read only a short ode. Where the "Nightingale," "Urn," and "Melancholy" odes left us with the contraries, "To Autumn" fulfills the promise of the "Ode to Psyche": to let the warm love in, to resolve contraries, because there is no further need for progression.

# The "Ode on Melancholy"

## Walter Jackson Bate

The "Ode on Melancholy" matches the "Nightingale" and the "Grecian Urn" in restrained intensity of language and versification. An important difference, however, is that it lacks a dominant symbol. Keats is therefore forced to storm the main gate of the subject directly. This was not a decisive handicap. He was used to it. Partly because of his lack of formal education and his early freedom from the self-consciousness it often creates, he had begun writing poetry in this way, reassured by the large directness of earlier poetry, and without thought of the "winding stair" which is often necessary, said Bacon, for rising. And alone among the major modern poets, Keats was able to get away with it. The ode "To Autumn" is a triumphant example. Yet, for over a year and a half, his ultimate ideal had been dramatic; and in the "Nightingale" and the "Grecian Urn" he had at last found himself developing a form of dramatic lyric that included symbolic debate. The burden of the "Ode on Melancholy" is carried by the massive last stanza in what again reminds us of Keats's direct credos: a richly complex credo now, distilling much that had been actively dramatized in the other odes, especially the "Nightingale." But a direct assertion of belief, whatever else may be said of it, can hardly be dramatic unless there is either some form of debate or else a developing discovery by the poet of what he really believes. Neither of these is present in the "Ode on Melancholy." Keats's own awareness of this may explain the unusual stance he decides to give the poem—unusual for him, however common otherwise: that in which

From *John Keats*. © 1963 by the President and Fellows of Harvard College. The Belknap Press of Harvard University Press, 1963.

the poet addresses an imaginary person with protest or exhortation. Wordsworth especially was fond of it, often turning it into what seems to be a form of hectoring ("Up! up! my Friend, and quit your books"); and it was doubtless one of the mannerisms of Wordsworth that Keats had in mind when he spoke of poetry that "bullies us" and, "if we do not agree, seems to put its hand in its breeches pocket." The mode was so alien to Keats's habitual thinking that no other poem he wrote uses the device in this direct way.

But he faced a practical problem. Given the feelings that were settling, with eloquence and strength, into the last two stanzas (for it is they that put what he really wishes to say), and lacking the obduracies of a dominant symbol that he can debate, how can the poem assume a length appropriate to the capacious stanza he is using and acquire movement and the presence of a living voice? The temptation was to introduce himself as if in debate with someone else: and in contrast with the opening of the other odes, the first stanza starts with abrupt protest:

> No, no, go not to Lethe, neither twist
> Wolf's-bane, tight-rooted, for its poisonous wine.

The protest of the first stanza is against the conventional symbols of oblivion, death, and melancholy. In this indirect presentation of the absent voice he wishes to answer, the stanza fails to progress, though the language is no less condensed than later. Instead, images conventionally associated with melancholy—he had been lately reading Burton's *Anatomy of Melancholy*—are simply piled upon the same point:

> Nor suffer thy pale forehead to be kiss'd
> By nightshade, ruby grape of Proserpine;
> Make not your rosary of yew-berries,
> Nor let the beetle, nor the death-moth be
> Your mournful Psyche, nor the downy owl
> A partner in your sorrow's mysteries;
> For shade to shade will come too drowsily,
> And drown the wakeful anguish of the soul.

The passing of shade to deeper shade, of twilight into night, will bring only the deadening of awareness. It is wakefulness that is prized, the capacity to savor, even if it include "wakeful anguish"—a heart, as he wrote in the "Grecian Urn," "high-sorrowful and cloy'd."

Anticipating the ode "To Autumn" of four months later, the second stanza then turns directly to the vivid acceptance of process. In the very springing of the flowers and the new green of the hill, transience falls upon them like a "shroud" as they emerge into being. But the same process in which death is implicit is also leading things into existence and fostering them toward fulfillment. This is an "April shroud," promising existence as well as death:

> But when the melancholy fit shall fall
> Sudden from heaven like a weeping cloud,
> That fosters the droop-headed flowers all,
> And hides the green hill in an April shroud;
> Then glut thy sorrow on a morning rose,
> Or on the rainbow of the salt sand-wave,
> Or on the wealth of globèd peonies;
> Or if thy mistress some rich anger shows,
> Emprison her soft hand, and let her rave,
> And feed deep, deep upon her peerless eyes.

Even if the objects at which we clutch were to remain as relatively impervious to process as the Grecian urn, we, in our own reactions, could not. "Where's the eye," as Keats wrote in the lines on "Fancy," that does not "weary"?

> Not a Mistress but doth cloy.
> Where's the cheek that doth not fade
> Too much gaz'd at?

Yet even if our feelings and their objects could continue to sustain each other, and we possessed an uninterrupted happiness—a "happiness carried to extreme," as he wrote George in April,

> What must it end in?—Death—and who in such a case could bear with death. . . . But in truth I do not believe in this sort of perfectibility—the nature of the world will not admit of it. . . . The point at which Man may arrive is as far as the parallel state in inanimate nature and no further—For instance suppose a rose to have sensation, it blooms on a beautiful morning it enjoys itself—but there comes a cold wind, a hot sun—it cannot escape it, it cannot destroy its annoyances—they are as native to the world as itself; no more can man be happy in spite, the world[l]y elements will prey upon his nature.

The knowledge both of our own brevity and the brevity of what we seek to hold awakens the drowsy, easily distracted attention, and fosters a heightened awareness that will match the transient process it salutes—an awareness that itself inevitably leads to the "sovran shrine" of melancholy. For it is not simply the knowledge of transience that brings sorrow or pain. In a response sufficiently intense—a response duplicating and identifying itself with the active process it acknowledges and shares—the full emotional resources of our nature are called into play. Pain and "aching pleasure" pass organically into each other as the nectar sipped by the bee passes into the poison sting within its body. Images of pleasure and pain are now coalesced in the final stanza. For the contrast now is not of one with the other but rather of both, in organic combination, with the dimly allegorical background (the "temple," "Veiled Melancholy" and her "sovran shrine," the "cloudy trophies")—allegorical images that Keats had once so warmly incorporated in narrative but that now (as later in the *Fall of Hyperion*) loom abstract and shadowlike, suggesting the permanence of the nonhuman:

> She dwells with Beauty—Beauty that must die;
>   And Joy, whose hand is ever at his lips
> Bidding adieu; and aching Pleasure nigh,
>   Turning to poison while the bee-mouth sips:
> Ay, in the very temple of Delight
>   Veil'd Melancholy has her sovran shrine,
>     Though seen of none save him whose strenuous tongue
>   Can burst Joy's grape against his palate fine;
> His soul shall taste the sadness of her might,
>     And be among her cloudy trophies hung.

# The Fierce Dispute: The "Ode to a Nightingale"

*Morris Dickstein*

We enter a different world when we move . . . [into] the tormented opening
stanzas of the "Ode to a Nightingale."

> My heart aches, and a drowsy numbness pains
> My sense, as though of hemlock I had drunk,
> Or emptied some dull opiate to the drains
> One minute past, and Lethe-wards had sunk.
>
> (1–4)

Without introduction we are propelled to the center of Keats's anguished
meditation on consciousness. We meet Keats in a drugged stupor, the
archetypal state of numbness and unconsciousness which has dogged him
since the early "Fill for me a brimming bowl," through the many versions
of "the feel of not to feel it." Every variant of that experience is here, and
the effect is one of reinforcement and accretion. (Compare the even more
explicit though more literary catalogue of what Keats wishes away at the
beginning of the "Ode on Melancholy.") "Drowsy numbness" suggests
not only affectlessness but sleep, once benign but now paradoxically painful
to his "sense" (i.e., mind as well as feeling). The mention of Lethe brings
in the old motif of "sweet forgetting," and the metaphorical hemlock adds
overtones of death, foreshadowing its later appearances in the poem.

In the fifth line Keats addresses the nightingale directly; in such a
state talk is therapy, a way of not going under. It is also an apology, for

---

From *Keats and His Poetry: A Study in Development.* © 1971 by the University of
Chicago. The University of Chicago Press, 1971.

as in the "Epistle to Reynolds" Keats's mood "spoils the singing of the Nightingale."

> 'Tis not through envy of thy happy lot,
>     But being too happy in thine happiness,—
>         That thou, light-winged Dryad of the trees,
>             In some melodious plot
>         Of beechen green, and shadows numberless,
>             Singest of summer in full-throated ease.
>                                                 (5–10)

The location of the nightingale (*pace* Brown) remains indeterminate, though as tree-dweller the bird seems for the moment close by. Still, between the poet and the nightingale there is a distance he had never experienced with the less resistant Psyche. Even so, Keats disclaims envious longing. He boasts of self-abnegating rather than covetous feelings; he suffers from excessive empathy, from being too happy for the bird. Immediately, ever so subtly, the happiness of the nightingale becomes ambiguous, associated as it is with the poet's painful numbness, and subject to self-destroying excess. It is happiness nonetheless, and it tells Keats of a summer world not yet present in nature, but the bird's visionary power leaves it in turn invisible (and inaccessible) among the "shadows numberless," disembodied into a "melodious plot" and into the "full-throated ease" of pure song.

In all this—including the qualifications, which we do not forget, even when Keats gives full sway to a desire to be united with the bird—the first stanza deftly introduces the various symbolic meanings of the bird. As a singer she suggests art, and as bird and Dryad she represents an aspect of nature. Yet she is an art already associated with airy uncertainty, distance and disembodiment—and by the second stanza, where wine becomes the true fountain of the Muses, with intoxication. Above all, as the poem goes on, the bird comes to signify an art free of self-consciousness and a nature free of tragic necessity, a nature that pits sensation and process *against* consciousness. From the perspective of our survey of Keats's development, his longing to join the nightingale, which becomes so intense in the second, third, and fourth stanzas, can only be seen retrospectively. The poet's desire to "fade far away, dissolve" and "leave the world unseen" powerfully sums up and reenacts the impulses toward self-annihilation and luxurious transcendence that played so predominant a part in his earlier poetry. "The viewless wings of Poesy" of the fourth stanza, like the intoxicating Hippocrene of the second, can only refer to the poesy of *Endymion* and the early poems, not to that newer conception of the imagination painstakingly developed in the *King Lear* sonnet, the letters, the third book of *Hyperion*, and the last stanza of the "Ode to Psyche." It is poetry as a visionary bower for the spirit, a refuge from the pains of selfhood and actuality, rather than a tragic poetry of self-knowledge and the widening of consciousness. Keats returns to these earlier impulses because they still move him, still represent a real idea of happiness and imagination for him. Where he has failed to exorcise them by simply setting them aside or transmuting them, he may succeed by giving them full expression, by bringing them into the light of consciousness and freshly exploring them. The synthesis of "Psyche" proves to have been too easily achieved; the self must undergo a new polarization, a new interior dialogue.

The stages of the dialectic in the first part of the poem are not difficult to distinguish. Keats describes a series of wavelike gestures toward self-dissolution and union with the bird. The first, for a moment all too successful, has taken place just before the poem begins. It has resulted, as Keats tells in the opening lines, not in the genuine extinction of self-consciousness but in what he elsewhere calls an "unpleasant numbness" that "does not take away the pain of existence" (1:287). Yet each wave sets in motion a countercurrent, as Keats's mind moves from bird to self and self to bird. From "being too happy in thine happiness" he sinks into the paralyzing condition described in the opening lines; in anatomizing that condition he draws his mind upward again toward the happy song of the nightingale. This leads to the second wave, as Keats imagines joining the bird through Bacchus. The terms of the dialectic now broaden and deepen; the song's "full-throated ease" becomes a foretaste of the completion and wholeness of summer. This leads Keats to dream of a delicious summer world of "Dance, and Provencal song, and sunburnt mirth," an ideal "warm South" of sensation without pain and imagination without consciousness. But the large gesture of the second stanza leads to the countermovement of the third. The attempt to flee to an idyllic world suddenly makes Keats all the more poignantly aware of the world of actuality which he is trying to escape. It is a world "where men sit and hear each other groan," that is, where the only community is one of pain, the exact opposite of the world of dance and song and mirth. It is a world in which suffering is magnified by the desperate consciousness of suffering:

> Where youth grows pale, and spectre-thin, and dies;
> Where but to think is to be full of sorrow
> And leaden-eyed despairs.
>
> (26–28)

It is a world of temporality in which all is perishable, all must change:

> Where beauty cannot keep her lustrous eyes,
>    Or new Love pine at them beyond to-morrow.
>
>                                    (29–30)

Clearly this second fantasy of union with the happy song of the bird has failed Keats even more dismally than the first. But out of his complete despair comes an equally powerful though strained new gesture of escape:

> Away! away! for I will fly to thee,
>    Not charioted by Bacchus and his pards,
> But on the viewless wings of Poesy,
>    Though the dull brain perplexes and retards.
>
>                                    (31–34)

What follows is perhaps the most lovely yet surely the most variously interpreted section of the poem. Some things are clear, however. No matter how we read "Already with thee!"—whether we follow Bate and others in assuming the poet to have achieved sudden though perhaps illusory union with the bird or agree with Wasserman that "such a reading can lead only to inconsistencies, if not to nonsense"—by the next line ("haply") and thereafter ("But here there is no light") the poet is separate from the bird. Keats for the moment settles for a lower paradise than that suggested by the song of the nightingale. He returns, as he had done in the "Ode to Psyche," to the favorite *topos* of the early poems, the bower. The poet's spirit has been sorely tried, and now the Poesy of *Endymion*, to which he has at last appealed at the beginning of the fourth stanza, responds with the bower vision that is its only cure, its best treasure. One key to the passage is the "embalmed darkness" which envelops the scene as Keats writes. "Balm" is a significant word in some of the bower scenes of *Endymion* as well. We are told that after the death of Adonis the love-sick Venus

> Heal'd up to the wound, and, with a balmy power,
> Medicined death to a lengthened drowsiness:
> The which she fills with visions, and doth dress
> In all this quiet luxury.
>
>                                    (2, 483–86)

Similarly, in the "golden clime" of Circe's den ("this arbitrary queen of sense"),

> every eve, nay every spendthrift hour
> Shed balmy consciousness within that bower.
>
>                                    (3, 465–66)

"Balmy consciousness" as opposed to a consciousness of pain; a balm which can heal death and yet, as "lengthened drowsiness," is a kind of death itself, the death of the mind for the sake of "visions" and sensuous "luxury." It is this death of the mind which Keats prays for when he addresses Sleep as the "soft embalmer of the still midnight" ("To Sleep").

In spite of its ancestry, this bower, like the one in the "Ode to Psyche," is fundamentally different from those in *Endymion*. In *Endymion* there is a simple polarity between the bower and the world, between vision and actuality, sensation and consciousness. In the "Ode to Psyche" Keats had sought to reconcile these antinomies, to refine and transform the bower by altering its regressive and infantile character. In the first four stanzas of the Nightingale ode the polarities are restated, definitively, one might say. In the fifth stanza, the closest in spirit to the "Ode to Psyche," Keats comes to rest for a moment on a middle ground, a lower paradise, in Geoffrey Hartman's words, "the middle-ground of imaginative activity, not reaching to vision, not falling into blankness." It is also a middle ground between "balmy consciousness" and thought, enjoyment and awareness. It is instructive to observe the effects of the darkness on this scene.

> I cannot see what flowers are at my feet,
>> Nor what soft incense hangs upon the boughs,
> But, in embalmed darkness, guess each sweet
>> (41–43)

The failure of sight seems to set Keats's other senses going more vividly, as such synaesthetic phrases as "soft incense" make clear. Yet also it sets the *mind's* eye functioning more intensely, for the mind, bereft of vision, must construct the whole scene from sheer *knowledge* of the natural world. (The timeless and symbolic Nature represented by the nightingale will not do here.) But this, like other dualities in the stanza, is only a germ, a suggestion that is important insofar as it is taken up in the next stanza, which is the real turning point of the poem. The fifth stanza, like the conclusion of the "Ode to Psyche," proves an unstable compound. The reflective mental activity in the stanza anticipates the new self-consciousness that appears in the sixth, just as the passive sensuousness of the "embalmed darkness" foreshadows the desire for "easeful Death." The polarities reassert themselves, for the purpose of confrontation rather than reconciliation.

The sixth stanza of the "Ode to a Nightingale" is perhaps the most significant moment in Keats's poetry, and one of the most important in all Romantic literature. It is foreshadowed as early as "Sleep and Poetry," when Keats sees the visionary car of the imagination, only to have it displaced by "a sense of real things" (157). It is the culminating moment of

Keats's lifelong struggle against consciousness, his quest for self-annihilation made all the more complicated by his strong commitment to "the thinking principle" and to the painful extension of self-knowledge. The logical conclusion of that desire for self-annihilation is the desire for death, the wish to be wholly free of the burdens of selfhood, a longing to which so many of the Romantics were willing prey.

> Darkling I listen; and, for many a time
>   I have been half in love with easeful Death,
> Call'd him soft names in many a mused rhyme,
>   To take into the air my quiet breath;
> Now more than ever seems it rich to die,
>   To cease upon the midnight with no pain,
>   While thou art pouring forth thy soul abroad
>     In such an ecstasy!
>
> (51–58)

The darkness of the bower leads to the thought of death, and death suddenly seems to be the only road by which Keats can make his last attempt to join the nightingale. Now the retrospective meaning of the whole poem becomes for the first time explicit. Keats is caught up not only in the desire to die but in a sudden brilliant awareness of the importance of that wish to the whole history of his imagination. At this point criticism, having long since rescued Keats from decadence and convinced itself of the essential "health" and "vitality" of his imagination, clears its throat uneasily and cites the convenient but enigmatic sonnet "Why did I laugh?" of which a verbal echo occurs in this stanza. Convenient too is Keats's own assurance to his brother and sister-in-law of his health and sanity in composing that sonnet: "it was written with no Agony but that of ignorance. . . . I went to bed, and enjoyed an uninterrupted sleep—Sane I went to bed and sane I arose" (2:81–82). The very need for such assurance, and his hesitation in sending them the poem, shows us how much Keats felt his balance threatened by the death wish. But that sonnet does not readily fit the specifications of this stanza. Keats insists, for one thing, on the recurrence and frequency of his longing ("many a time . . . in many a mused rhyme"). Furthermore, he describes it in erotic terms, which bring to mind not "Why did I Laugh?" but the oft-repeated desire of the early Keats to "die a death / Of luxury," to experience "richer entanglements, enthralments far / More self-destroying," when the self is entirely sloughed off and "our state / Is like a floating spirit's."

Keats had already, in the third stanza, enviously praised the nightingale for its ignorance of the harsh world of actuality. He had longed to

> Fade far away, dissolve, and quite forget
>   What thou among the leaves hast never known,
> The weariness, the fever, and the fret.
>                                        (21–23)

He had felt himself trapped by self-consciousness, in a world "where but to think is to be full of sorrow / And leaden-eyed despairs." Now Keats restates the innocence of the nightingale in positive terms, as an experience of perpetual self-transcendence. It is "pouring forth [its] soul abroad / In such an ecstasy!"—literally, in separation from itself. This desire for self-transcendence is the basis of Keats's death wish: the nightingale exists wholly within the terms of his own inner conflict.

At this point the poem turns. His association of the thought of death with the song of the now transcendent nightingale seems an incongruity;

> Still thou wouldst sing, and I have ears in vain—
>   To thy high requiem become a sod.
>                                        (59–60)

The thought of real death intervenes, not "easeful Death . . . To cease upon the midnight with no pain," but to "become a sod," a clod, a piece of earth. The song of the nightingale, no longer happy, now becomes a "high requiem" sung over the oblivious corpse of the all-too-human poet. Death is not a fulfillment, a luxury or a transcendent passage, but simply the end. At this recognition an unbridgeable abyss opens up between the poet and the nightingale.

> Thou wast not born for death, immortal Bird!
>   No hungry generations tread thee down.
>                                        (61–62)

The tone of this seventh stanza is different from that of the third, which had made a similar statement. The description of man's condition is comparable, and the bird remains blissfully free of it, but there is now no sickly pathos in Keats's tone and no envy in his view of the nightingale. The spell of the bird's song has begun to relax its hold on him; he is becoming, quite literally, dis-enchanted.

In the third stanza, most of the images of suffering were unconvincing ("Here, where men sit and hear each other groan; / Where palsy shakes a few, sad, last gray hairs"). Keats seemed to be glancing at everyday reality

over his shoulder, in the act of fleeing from it, with no will to confront it
or even observe it concretely. Something decisive has intervened between
those images and that of the "hungry generations" or Ruth, "sick for
home," standing "in tears amid the alien corn." The palsied old men and
spectre-thin youths of the third stanza are just victims, and pathetic ones.
The "hungry generations" are both victims and agents: they do the treading
too, though they themselves are eventually trod upon.

We are reminded, in spite of the difference of emphasis, of the message
of Oceanus to his fellow Titans:

> "So on our heels a fresh perfection treads,
> A power more strong in beauty, born of us
> And fated to excel us."
>
> (*Hyperion*, 2, 212–14)

The message of Oceanus, which is central to *Hyperion*, has a special rele-
vance to the concluding idea of the "Ode to a Nightingale," especially in
this seventh stanza. His speech is usually read as an expression of cosmic
optimism, and indeed it does assert a belief in progress. Yet the central
doctrine of the speech is almost tragic. Oceanus informs the shattered Saturn
of the law of mutability and transience: "Thou art not the beginning nor
the end" (2, 190). Though he uses sometimes cosmic and sometimes natural
terms, his message is no more or less than a philosophy of history—history
rather than accident, history rather than myth: "We fall by course of Nature's law, not force / Of thunder, or of Jove" (2, 181–82). Saturn, however, being king of the gods, has been "blind from sheer supremacy" (2,
185). A figure of myth, he had ruled over a world of apparent mythic
permanence. What Oceanus explains to him is the action of the first two
books of the poem: his fall from myth into history (a fall whose effect, as
we have seen, is one of humanization). He tells Saturn of the simultaneous
"creations and destroyings" of history, and calls for a tragic acceptance free
of self-delusion:

> "to bear all naked truths,
> And to envision circumstance, all calm,
> That is the top of sovereignty."
>
> (2, 203–5)

In the sixth stanza of the ode Keats suddenly confronts the "naked
truth" about death, which separates the human self of the poet from the
visionary song of the nightingale. As a result a vast distance begins to open
out between the poet and the bird. In his disenchantment with the bird

Keats moves from myth to history. He situates himself firmly on "this passing night," in the endless procession of the "hungry generations." The nightingale's song, which a moment earlier he had envied as a sign of ecstatic self-transcendence, now becomes merely "self-same," which suggests that it is not only identical at all periods of history but also, unlike the poet, self-less. For Keats the recognition of this difference is not depressing, as in the third stanza, but challenging. The difference between the third and seventh stanzas is akin to the difference between Saturn and Oceanus, the one stunned, bereft of his mythic "identity" and therefore of the will to live, the other announcing to Saturn "the pain of truth, to whom 'tis pain" (2, 202), by which the individual may hope to endure. Endurance is the subject of the seventh stanza, as death was of the sixth, but it is not only the immortal nightingale that endures. Beyond the transhistorical permanence of the nightingale is the more tenuous but relevant seizure of life of the human agent within tragedy: that of the "hungry generations," or that of the poet who can choose at last to fall out of love with death, or that of the bereaved and exiled Ruth, who is taught by her mother-in-law to begin life anew, and is rewarded by becoming the mother of a dynasty.

Readers who ignore the implicit but growing disenchantment of the poet with the nightingale, who see it merely, if at all, as an increasing distance, are likely to be unpleasantly jarred by the conclusion of the seventh stanza and by the final stanza that follows. Keats describes the song as

> The same that oft-times hath
> Charm'd magic casements, opening on the foam
> Of perilous seas, in faery lands forlorn.
> (68–70)

To E. C. Pettet the word "forlorn" even if "taken with the minimum of emotional tone . . . is certainly a strange one to be attached to a dream and a sort of poetry that Keats had always regarded with such unqualified imaginative delight." He even wonders whether "the word slipped in without much consideration as an easy, sound-pleasing, alliterative rhyme to finish the stanza." This disregards the pointed emphasis that Keats puts on the word when he uses it as a bridge to the concluding stanza. It ignores the rejection of romance that had been foreshadowed as early as the last two books of *Endymion*, and announced programmatically in the sonnet on *Lear*. Now, in his most completely retrospective poem, a genuine poem of conversion and self-definition, Keats associates the song of the nightingale with the poetry of romance, with the "poesy" perhaps of his own long "Poetic Romance." For the nightingale has already been identified with that aspect of romance which Keats had always singled out over all others, escape, and in the end it is escape that Keats mainly wishes to reject.

Among professional critics there are two broad groups that have usually chosen to ignore or deemphasize this rejection. The older critics, still attached to the nineteenth-century image of an aesthete cultivating beauty and sensation for their own sake, could hardly have been responsive to Keats's final disenchantment with the nightingale. Thus Bridges and Garrod single out for censure the description of the song in the last stanza as a "plaintive anthem." More recently some writers, heirs in a special way of the doctrine of *l'art pour l'art*, have stressed the visionary side of Romantic poetry, the creation of autonomous imaginative worlds free of the inhibiting immediacies of self-consciousness and actuality. No poem is a more purposeful refutation of such an emphasis than the "Ode to a Nightingale," which is among other things an account of how immediate experience and radical self-awareness intervene in a Romantic poem to challenge and alter its mythicizing direction. Professor Wasserman, who reifies the visionary and self-annihilating impulses of the early Keats into doctrine, which he then applies to the greater poems, writes a long and revealing chapter on this ode. He reads the poem closely, but only to quarrel with it at every turn, to wish it different. Professor McLuhan, in his interesting essay on the odes, refuses to impute escapism to the early part of the poem, or even to the death wish of the sixth stanza. He speaks of "the paradox that ideal or disembodied beauty is richer in ontological content than actual life with its defeats and deprivations and 'leaden-eyed despairs.' " It is for this reason, he says, that "the stark negation of death is viewed as a positive good ('rich to die'), not so much as an evasion of difficulties as a seemingly easy means of transmuting the leaden stuff of life into glorious beauty." Professor Bloom, reading backward from the work of Wallace Stevens, praises the poem for

> giving the sense of the human making the choice of a human self, aware of its deathly nature, and yet having the will to celebrate the imaginative richness of mortality. The *Ode to a Nightingale* is the first poem to know and declare, wholeheartedly, that death is the mother of beauty.

Each of these interpretations contains some truth but all must come to grief on the last twenty-two lines of the poem. The "Ode to a Nightingale" is a tragic poem rather than a visionary one, founded like so many of the best Romantic poems not on imaginative flight but rather on the dialectical tension of the poet's divided self. But Keats, who could so readily luxuriate in his own inner tensions, here drives onward towards a tentative resolution. The seventh stanza ends on a note of surprise and paradox, "faery lands forlorn," but Keats concludes with a stanza of epilogue that explicitly reverses his longing for the nightingale and for all the deceptions of fancy that the nightingale has come to represent.

> Forlorn! the very word is like a bell
> To toll me back from thee to my sole self!
> Adieu! the fancy cannot cheat so well
> As she is fam'd to do, deceiving elf.
> Adieu! adieu! thy plaintive anthem fades
> Past the near meadows, over the still stream,
> Up the hill-side; and now 'tis buried deep
> In the next valley-glades:
> Was it a vision, or a waking dream?
> Fled is that music:—Do I wake or sleep?

Nothing could be more decisive than the characterization of the nightingale as a "deceiving elf," not even the phrase at the parallel point in the "Ode on a Grecian Urn": "Cold Pastoral!" Keats at last takes up residence, as he has repeatedly promised, in the difficult domain of the "sole self." There is a note of loss here, for as McLuhan points out there is something funereal in the tolling bell of the opening lines. But surely the primary meaning is of an awakening to life; "forlorn" serves as the bell that brings us back from the dreamworld of the nightingale and from the faery lands. It is rather the immortal nightingale who paradoxically dies, whose now "plaintive" song "fades" away and is "buried deep" in the next valley. (The song of course does not really change: it is the poet's response that turns it from a happy song of summer to a "high requiem" and finally to a "plaintive anthem," as if the bird were in the end aware of the poet's desertion.)

Yet for all the decisiveness of this epilogue, the poem ends on a knife-edge of uncertainty. In the last two lines Keats asks himself whether the departure of the nightingale represents a fall from vision into blankness—as in "Sleep and Poetry," where the "sense of real things . . . like a muddy stream, would bear along / My soul to nothingness" (157–59)—or whether it constitutes the emergence from a dreamworld into the reality of actual life? In the final line, much more distinctly than in the two opening lines of the stanza, we hear a genuine note of regret: "Fled is that music." A few months later, referring to another music which he had left behind, that of *Paradise Lost*, Keats would say that "I have but lately stood on my guard against Milton. Life to him would be death to me" (2:212). Like his tutelage to Milton, Keats's enchantment with the song of the nightingale had in the end turned into a struggle for survival. The bird, which would have presided over the poet's "easeful Death," has itself died; Keats is recalled to life, yet bids the bird farewell with a sense of bereavement.

Keats's final judgement is a balanced one, but the whole last part of the poem contains an emphasis opposite from that of "Sleep and Poetry" and *Endymion*. It is simply not true that for Keats, as Paul de Man asserts, "the condition of the 'sole self' is one of intolerable barrenness, the opposite of all that imagination, poetry and love can achieve. The experience of being 'tolled back to one's sole self' is always profoundly negative." This is the case in *Endymion*, where "the journey homeward to habitual self" (2, 276) is always painful, though, significantly, even there a journey Keats always insists on making. De Man feels that even the "Ode to a Nightingale" gives evidence of Keats's continued fear of self-confrontation. "The 'I' of the Nightingale Ode," he says, ". . . is always seen in a movement that takes it away from its own center." But that describes only the movement of the first part of the poem. The poem as a whole moves toward the final exorcising of that fear. Yet it is an exorcism which, given Keats's temperament, must be perpetually reenacted: only thus can we explain the history of his poetry from the *Lear* sonnet to the odes, and even the relation of the odes to each other.

# In the Shadow of Milton:
## The "Ode to Psyche"

*Harold Bloom*

Internalization of the precursor is the ratio I have elsewhere called *apophrades*, and in psychoanalysis it is hardly distinguishable from introjection. To trope upon a trope is to internalize it, so that aesthetic internalization seems very close to the kind of allusiveness that Milton perfected, the Romantics inherited, and Joyce brought to a new perfection in our century. Yet conflicts can be internalized also, and the Freudian theory of the superego seems dependent upon the notion that a father's authority can be internalized by the superego. Romantic internalization, as I have shown in another study, "The Internalization of Quest Romance," takes place primarily in intra-subjective terms, the conflict being between opposing principles *within the ego*. Further internalization, then, may aid in freeing a poet from superego-anxieties (the constraints perhaps of religious or moral tradition) or from ambivalence towards himself, but it is not of any initiatory use as a defense against precursors or id-anxieties, though it does enter into the final phase of the influence-struggle. Keats, who programmatically internalizes his themes in the "Ode to Psyche" and afterwards, is therefore peculiarly and overtly conscious of the anxiety of influence, even for a strong poet of the second Romantic generation. I suspect that is why the "Ode to Psyche," a profoundly self-discovering poem, follows the map of misprision more rigorously than all but a few other poems. Each of "Psyche" 's first four stanzas emphasizes one ratio in turn, with the fifth and last stanza dividing almost equally between the two final ratios. Keats does not displace his

From *A Map of Misreading*. © 1975 by Oxford University Press, Inc.

Miltonic-Wordsworthian model in any formal way, but relies entirely upon finding fresh imaginative space within himself.

The gently ironic opening stanza seems at first directed against the start of *Lycidas*, and certainly Keats's high good humor is maintained throughout; but the irony is a personal defense also. Keats gives us images of a surprising presence, of a Psyche "wingèd" and so divine, yet also reunited with Cupid here upon earth. But allusiveness is internalized in this opening *illusio*, and Keats hints that his role as *voyeur* is surprisingly close to that of Milton's Satan. He "Saw two fair creatures, couchèd side by side," just as Satan saw how our first parents "Straight side by side were laid, nor turn'd I ween / Adam from his fair Spouse . . . ," and just as the angel Gabriel some fifty lines later told his subordinates to "leave unsearcht no nook / But chiefly where those two fair Creatures lodge." In some sense Keats says Cupid and Psyche but means Adam and Eve; and in some sense he condemns himself for sharing Satan's lust of the eye, though again the self-condemnation is surely not wholly serious.

But the poetic dilemma is quite serious. Psyche is a belated goddess, and Keats is a belated poet, which is why the synecdoche of the second stanza culminates in so excited a recognition of Psyche, for this is also a moment of poetic self-recognition in which Keats discovers his true muse, though in a gently idealized form, not the grandly purgatorial form she will assume as Moneta in *The Fall of Hyperion*. The reunited lovers, Cupid and Psyche, are an image of the wholeness that Keats's mature poetry will seek.

In the next stanza, Keats reduces mythology to a metonymic catalog of emptiness, and though the reduction is remarkable light in tone, it has a defensive element nevertheless, for its motive is to deprecate poetic earliness, through the process of isolation. From so good-natured a nadir, one might not expect a strongly daemonic recovery to rise, yet Keats does achieve a Sublime of brightness until he can utter the wonderful hyperbole: "I see, and sing, by my own eyes inspired." With the single change of "no" to "thy" he proceeds to rescue the particulars of mythological worship from the fragmentary discontinuity into which he had broken them in the previous stanza:

> So let me be thy choir, and make a moan
>     Upon the midnight hours;
> Thy voice, thy lute, thy pipe, thy incense sweet
>     From swingèd censer teeming;
> Thy shrine, thy grove, thy oracle, thy heat
>     Of pale-mouthed prophet dreaming.

The heightening here is conveyed more through intensity of tone than through image, but the defense of repression is so finely obvious as to make commentary redundant. In the metaphor that follows, the familiar Romantic conceit of an internalized nature almost transcends its perspectivizing limitations, so extraordinary is Keats's art:

> Yes, I will be thy priest, and build a fane
>> In some untrodden region of my mind,
> Where branchèd thoughts, new grown with pleasant pain,
>> Instead of pines shall murmur in the wind:
> Far, far around shall those dark-clustered trees
>> Fledge the wild-ridgèd mountains steep by steep;
> And there by zephyrs, streams, and birds, and bees,
>> The moss-lain Dryads shall be lulled to sleep.

Internalization has taken him where he has not been before, and it is always a surprise to realize that this landscape, and this oxymoronic intensity, are wholly inside his psyche. The landscape is Wordsworthian, and the sublimation of a surrendered outside nature would seem to be complete, particularly with the beautiful but defeated image of the wood nymphs reclining on banks of moss, a pastoral sensuality that by being altogether mental suggests a realistic erotic despair. Keats completes the poem with a superb rhetoricity that substitutes for the earlier refrain of "too late," yet does so all too knowingly to be self-deceived:

> And in the midst of this wide quietness
> A rosy sanctuary will I dress
> With the wreathed trellis of a working brain,
>> With buds, and bells, and stars without a name,
> With all the gardener Fancy e'er could feign,
>> Who breeding flowers, will never breed the same:
> And there shall be for thee all soft delight
>> That shadowy thought can win,
> A bright torch, and a casement ope at night,
>> To let the warm Love in!

There is past time here, in the anterior feignings of the gardener Fancy, and there is a promised future, where Keats may substitute himself for the warm Cupid, but clearly there is no present time whatsoever. Keats projects the past as feigning and introjects the future as love, but even as there is no present moment so there is no place of presence, nor perhaps will there ever be. The Wordsworthian "wide quietness" and "shadowy thought" allude to the "shadowy ground" of man's mind that Wordsworth had proclaimed as the main region of his song in the "Recluse" fragment, part of which Keats had read as the "Prospectus" to *The Excursion*. What does Keats promise his Psyche? An earliness to wed her earliness, a bright torch to match her "brightest" that began the fourth stanza; but what is the reality of such earliness? Keats honestly gives only to take away, for how soft a delight can shadowy thought win? The open casement, as in line 69 of the "Ode to a Nightingale," is the genuine promise of earliness, and yet here as there it alludes transumptively to the Spenserian world of romance. Few poems are as persuasive as the "Ode to Psyche" is in its interpretation of its precursors; and few poems know so much about themselves and are able to complete themselves despite such knowledge.

# Poem and Ideology:
## A Study of Keats's "To Autumn"

*Geoffrey H. Hartman*

"Most English great poems have little or nothing to say." Few do that nothing so perfectly, one is tempted to add, as Keats's "To Autumn." Our difficulty as interpreters is related to the way consciousness almost disappears into the poem: the mind, for once, is not what is left (a kind of sublime litter) after the show is over. "To Autumn" seems to absorb rather than extrovert that questing imagination whose breeding fancies, feverish overidentifications, and ambitious projects motivate the other odes.

It is not that we lack the terms to describe the poem. On the contrary, as W. J. Bate has said, "for no other poem of the last two centuries does the classical critical vocabulary prove so satisfying." We can talk of its decorum, "the parts . . . contributing directly to the whole, with nothing left dangling or independent," of its lack of egotism, "the poet himself . . . completely absent; there is no 'I', no suggestion of the discursive language that we find in the other odes," and finally of a perfect concreteness or adequacy of symbol, the union in the poem of ideal and real, of the "greeting of the Spirit" and its object.

Yet terms like these point to an abstract perfection, to something as pure of content as a certain kind of music. They bespeak a triumph of form that exists but not—or not sufficiently—the nature of that form: its power to illumine experience, to cast a new light, a new shadow maybe, on things. In what follows I suggest, daringly, that "To Autumn" has something to say: that it is an ideological poem whose very form expresses a national

---

From *Literary Theory and Structure.* © 1973 by Yale University. Yale University Press, 1973.

45

idea and a new stage in consciousness, or what Keats himself once called the "gregarious advance" and "grand march of intellect."

There are problems with *ideological*, a word whose meaning is more charged in Marxist than in general usage. Marxism thinks of ideology as a set of ideas that claim universality while serving a materialistic or class interest. "Ideology is untruth, false consciousness, lie. It shows up in failed words of art . . . and is vulnerable to criticism. . . . Art's greatness consists in allowing that to be uttered which ideology covers up." The attack on ideology in Marxism resembles that on "unearned abstractions" in Anglo-American formalistic theory, except that it engages in "depth politics" to uncover these abstractions. Formalistic criticism can worry overt ideas or idealisms, Keats's "Beauty is Truth, Truth Beauty," for example, yet it accepts gladly the disappearance of ideas, or disinterestedness of form in "To Autumn." There is no attempt to demystify this form by discovering behind its decorum a hidden interest. In a low-risk theory of this kind the presence of ideas can be disturbing but not, obviously, their absence.

The great interpretive systems we know of have all been interest-centered, however; they have dug deep, mined, undermined, removed the veils. The Synagogue is blind to what it utters, the Church understands. The patient dreams, the doctor translates the dream. The distant city is really our city; the *unheimlich* the *heim-lich*; strange, uncanny, and exotic are brought home. Like those etymologies older scholars were so fond of, which showed us the fossilized stem of abstract words, so everything is slain, in interest-theories, on the stem of generational or class conflict.

Yet like nature itself, which has so far survived man's use of it, art is not polluted by such appropriations. Some works may be discredited, others deepened—the scandal of form remains. From Kant through Schopenhauer and Nietzsche, the aesthetic element proper is associated with disinterestedness, impersonality, and resistance to utilitarian concepts. Beauty of this undetermined kind becomes an itch: the mind, says Empson, wants to scratch it, to see what is really there, and this scratching we call interpretation. Most men, says Schopenhauer, seek in objects "only some relation to their will, and with everything that has not such a relation there sounds within them, like a ground-bass, the constant, inconsolable lament, 'It is of no use to me.' " Though the link between art and impersonality is often acknowledged—in New Criticism as well as Neoclassic theory—no very successful *interpretive* use of the principle exists. The notion of impersonality is vulnerable because so easily retranslated into unconscious interest or the masked presence of some *force majeure*.

I try to face this problem of the ideology of form by choosing a poem without explicit social context and exploring its involvement in social and historical vision. This would be harder, needless to say, if Keats had not elsewhere explicitly worried the opposition of dreamer and poet or poet and thinker. Even if "To Autumn" were a holiday of the spirit, some workday concerns of the poet would show through. My use of the concept of ideology, at the same time, will seem halfway or uncritical to the Marxist thinker. In uncovering Keats's ideology I remain as far as possible within terms provided by Keats himself, or furnished by the ongoing history of poetry. This is not, I hope, antiquarianism, but also not transvaluation. It should be possible to consider a poem's *geschichtlicher Stundenschlag* (Adorno)—how it tells the time of history—without accepting a historical determinism. Keats's poetry is indeed an event in history: not in world-history, however, but simply in the history of fiction, in our awareness of the power and poverty of fictions.

My argument runs that "To Autumn," an ode that is hardly an ode, is best defined as an English or Hesperian model which overcomes not only the traditional type of sublime poem but the "Eastern" or epiphanic consciousness essential to it. The traditional type was transmitted by both Greek and Hebrew religious poetry, and throughout the late Renaissance and eighteenth century, by debased versions of the Pindaric or cult hymn. Only one thing about epiphanic structure need be said now: it evokes the presence of a god, or vacillates sharply between imagined presence and absence. Its rhetoric is therefore a crisis-rhetoric, with priest or votary, vastation or rapture, precarious nearness or hieratic distance ("Ah Fear! Ah frantic Fear! I see, I see thee near!"). As these verses by William Collins suggest, epiphanic structure proceeds by dramatic turns of mood and its language is ejaculative (Lo, Behold, O come, O see). Keats's "Hesperianism" triumphs, in "To Autumn," over this archaic style with its ingrained, superstitious attitude toward power—power seen as external and epochal. The new sublimity domesticates with the heart; the poet's imagination is neither imp nor incubus. Though recognizably sublime, "To Autumn" is a poem of *our* climate.

Climate is important. It ripens wits as well as fruits, as Milton said in another context. The higher temperature and higher style of the other odes are purged away: we have entered a temperate zone. What is grown here, this "produce of the air," is like its ambience: Hesperian art rather than oriental ecstasy or unnatural flight of the imagination. Autumn is clearly a mood as well as a season, and Stevens would have talked about a weather of the mind. Yet "mood" and "weather" have an aura of changeableness, even of volatility, while the Autumn ode expresses something firmer: not, as so often in Stevens or in the "Beulah" moments of other poets, a note among notes but, as in Spenser, a vast cloud-region or capability. The very shape of the poem—firm and regular without fading edges but also no overdefined contours—suggests a slowly expanding constellation that moves as a whole, if it moves at all.

Its motion is, in fact, part of the magic. Time lapses so gently here; we pass from the fullness of the maturing harvest to the stubble plains without experiencing a cutting edge. If time comes to a point in "To Autumn" it is only at the end of the poem, which verges (more poignant than pointed) on a last "gathering." The scythe of time, the sense of mortality, the cutting of life into distinct, epochal phases is not felt. We do not even stumble into revelation, however softly—there is no moment which divides before and after as in the "Ode to Psyche" with its supersoft epiphany, its Spenserian and bowery moment which makes the poet Psyche's devotee despite her "shadowy thought" nature. The Autumn ode is nevertheless a *poesis*, a shaped segment of life coterminous with that templar "region of the mind" which the other poems seek, though they may honor more insistently the dichotomy of inside and out, fane and profane. Poetry, to change "the whole habit of the mind," changes also our view of the mind's habitat. To say the "To Autumn" is ideological and that its pressure of form is "English" has to do with that also.

I begin with what is directly observable, rather than with curious knowledge of archaic ode or hymn. In the odes of Keats there is a strong, clearly marked moment of disenchantment, or of illusion followed by disillusion. Fancy, that "Queen of shadows" (Charlotte Smith), becomes a "deceiving elf"—and although the deception remains stylized, and its shock releases pathos rather than starker sentiments, it is as pointed as the traditional turn of the Great Ode. (Compare the turn, for example, from one mode of music to another in Dryden's *Alexander's Feast* or the anastrophe "He is not dead, he lives" in pastoral elegy.) The transition leading from stanzas 7 to 8 in the Nightingale ode is such a turn, which results in calling imagination a "deceiving elf." An imaginative fancy that has sustained itself despite colder thoughts is farewelled.

There is, exceptionally, no such turn in "To Autumn." The poem starts on enchanted ground and never leaves it. This special quality becomes even clearer when we recall that "La Belle Dame sans Merci," with its harvest background and soft ritual progression, ends in desolation of spirit on the cold hillside. But because the final turn of the Nightingale ode, though clear as a bell, is not gross in its effect, not productive of coital sadness, a comparison with Autumn's finale is still possible. In "To Autumn" birds are preparing to fly to a warmer clime, a "visionary south," though we do not see them leave or the cold interrupt. In "To a Nightingale" the poet is allowed a call—adieu, adieu—which is birdlike still and colors the darker "forlorn," while his complete awakening is delayed ("Do I wake or sleep?") and verbal prolongations are felt. There is no complete disenchantment even here.

"To Autumn," moreover, can be said to have something approaching a strophic turn as we enter the last stanza. With "Where are the songs of Spring? Aye, where are they?" a plaintive anthem sounds. It is a case, nevertheless, where a premise is anticipated and absorbed. The premise is that of transience, or the feel of winter, and the rest of the stanza approaches that cold threshold. The premise is absorbed because its reference is back to Spring instead of forward to Winter; by shifting from eye to ear, to the music-theme, Keats enriches Autumn with Spring. We remain within a magical circle where things repeat each other in finer tone, as Autumn turns into a second Spring: "While barred clouds *bloom* the soft-dying day." The music now heard is no dirge of the year but a mingling of lullaby and aubade. For the swallows a second summer is at hand (aubade). For us— if we cannot follow them any more than the elusive nightingale—what comes next is not winter but night (lullaby). We go gently off, in either case, on extended wings.

Thus "To Autumn," like Stevens's "Sunday Morning," becomes oddly an Ode to Evening. The full meaning of this will appear. But in terms of formal analysis we can say that the poem has no epiphany or decisive turn or any absence/presence dialectic. It has, instead, a *westerly drift* like the sun. Each stanza, at the same time, is so equal in its poetical weight, so loaded with its own harvest, that westering is less a natural than a poetic state—it is a mood matured by the poem itself. "To Autumn," in fact, does not explicitly evolve from sunrise to sunset but rather from a rich to a clarified dark. Closely read it starts and ends in twilight. "Season of mists and mellow fruitfulness"—though the mists are of the morning, the line links fertility and semidarkness in a way that might be a syntactical accident were it not for the more highly developed instance of "I cannot see what flowers are at my feet . . . ," that famous stanza from the Nightingale ode where darkened senses also produce a surmise of fruitfulness. The Autumn ode's twilight is something inherent, a condition not simply of growth but of imaginative growth. Westering here is a spiritual movement, one that tempers visionariness into surmise and the lust for epiphany into finer-toned repetitions. We do not find ourselves in a temple but rather in Tempe "twixt sleepe and wake." We can observe the ode unfolding as a self-renewing surmise of fruitfulness: as waking dream or "widening speculation" rather than nature-poem and secularized hymn.

Concerning *surmise*: I have suggested elsewhere its importance for Romantic poetry, how it hovers between factual and fantastic. Its presence is often marked by a "magic casement" effect: as in Wordsworth's "Solitary Reaper," a window opens unexpectedly on a secret or faraway scene.

> No nightingale did ever chaunt
> More welcome notes to weary bands
> Of travellers in some shady haunt,
> Among Arabian sands:

Keats has the interesting habit of interpreting pictures (usually imaginary) as scenes beheld from a magic window of this kind. Yet since the frame of the window is also the frame of the picture, he finds himself on an ambiguous threshold, intimately near yet infinitely removed from the desired place. Most of the odes are a feverish quest to enter the life of a pictured scene, to be totally where the imagination is. In the Autumn ode, however, there is no effort to cross a magic threshold: though its three stanzas are like a composite picture from some Book of Hours, we are placed so exactly at the bourn of the invisible picture window that the frame is not felt, nor the desperate haunting of imagination to get in. There is no precipitous "Already with thee" and no stylized dejection.

Something, perhaps, is lost by this: the sense of dangerous transition, of consciousness opening up, of a frozen power unsealing. But the ode remains resolutely meditative. When important images of transition occur they are fully *composed* and no more vibrant than metrical enjambments: "And sometimes like a gleaner thou dost keep / Steady thy laden head." Or, "Sometimes whoever seeks may find / Thee sitting careless." Strictly construed the "sometimes" goes here both with the seeking and with the finding: it is factored out and made prepositional. This is a framing device which further augments the feeling of surmise, of lighthearted questing. What reverberates throughout, and especially in this image of the gleaner, the most pictorial of the poem, is a light but steady pondering. It is not a pondering, of course, devoid of all tension: "keep / Steady," understood as a performative or "cozening imperative," suggests that the poet is not so much describing as urging the image on, in-feeling it. Let us follow this picture-pondering from verse to verse.

The opening stanza is so strongly descriptive, so loaded with told riches, that there seems to be no space for surmise. A desire to fill every rift with Autumns's gold produces as rich a banquet as Porphyro's heap of delicates in "The Eve of St. Agnes." Thesaurus stanzas of this kind are self-delighting in Keats; but they also have a deeper reason. Porphyro knows that Madeline will find reality poorer than her dream and enhances his value by serving himself up this way. The sumptuous ploy is to help him melt into his lady's waking thought. So Autumn's banquet, perhaps, intends to hold the awakening consciousness and allow the dream to linger. Not only the bees are deceived; the dream "Warm days will never cease" is not in them alone; it is already in Autumn, in her "conspiring." On this phrase all the rich, descriptive details depend; they are infinitives not indicatives, so that we remain in the field of mind. "Conspiring how to load and bless . . . To bend with apples . . . fill all fruit . . . To swell the gourd." As we move through Autumn's thought to the ripening of that thought, we cease to feel her as an external agent.

Thus, the descriptive fullness of the first stanza turns out to be thought-full as well: its pastoral furniture is a golden surmise, imagination in her most deliberate mood. By moving the point of view inward, Keats makes these riches mental riches, imaginative projects. He does not, at the same time, push the mental horizon to infinity: the mood remains infinitive, looking onto "something evermore about to be."

Once we see that what is being satisfied is empathy or in-feeling, and that to satisfy it Keats (like Autumn) fills outside with more and more inside, the structure of the poem as a progressive surmise becomes clear. In-feeling, in Keats, is always on the point of overidentifying; and even here it demands more than the first stanza's dream of truth. However glowing a prospect Autumn paints, it must still, as it were, come alive. This happens in the second stanza where the drowsy ponderer meets us in person. Now we are in the landscape itself; the harvest is now. The figure of Autumn amid her store is a moving picture, or the dream personified. Yet the two stanzas are perfectly continuous; in-feeling is still being expressed as the filling-up of a space—a figure like Autumn's was needed to plump the poem. Though we approach epiphanic personification in the figure of Autumn, the casualness of "sometimes" "sometimes," together with the easy mood of the opening question, gives us a sense of "widening speculation" and prevents a more than cornucopial view of the goddess.

But the dream is almost shattered at the end of the stanza. The word "oozings" extends itself phonically into "hours by hours," a chime that leads to the idea of transience in "Where are the songs of Spring?" Though immediately reabsorbed, this muted ubi sunt introduces the theme of mutability. Oozings—hours—ubi sunt. . . . A single word, or its echoes, might have disenchanted Keats like the turn on "forlorn" in the Nightingale ode. Disenchantment, however, does not occur: there is no reverse epiphany as in "La Belle Dame sans Merci," no waking into emptiness.

We have reached, nevertheless, the airiest of the stanzas. Does a chill wind not brush us, an airiness close to emptiness? Do we not anticipate the "cold hill's side"? Even if the mood of surmise is sustained, it might well be a surmise of death rather than fruitfulness.

Here, at the consummate point of Keats's art, in-feeling achieves its subtlest act. Keats conspires with Autumn to fill even the air. Air becomes a granary of sounds, a continuation of the harvest, or *Spätlese*. In this last and softest stanza, the ear of the ear is ripened.

More than a tour de force or finely sustained idea is involved. For at the end of other odes we find an explicit *cry*, which is part of their elegiac envoi. Here that cry is uttered, as it were, by the air itself, and can only be heard by an ear that knows how to glean such sounds. What is heard, to quote the modern poet closest to Keats,

> is not a cry of divine attention,
> Nor the smoke-drift of puffed-out heroes, nor human cry.
> It is the cry of leaves that do not transcend themselves.

In lyric poetry the cry is a sign of subjective feelings breaking through and in the cult-hymn of being possessed by divine power. It signifies in both a transcendence absent from this "final finding of the air." Lyricism, in "To Autumn," frees itself for once of elegy and ecstasy: it is neither a frozen moment of passion nor the inscription that prolongs it.

The Grecian urn's "Beauty is Truth, Truth Beauty" remains an extroverted, lapidary cry. However appropriate its philosophy, its form is barely snatched from a defeat of the imagination. "To Autumn" has no defeat in it. It is the most negative capable of all of Keats's great poems. Even its so-called death-stanza expresses no rush toward death, no clasping of darkness as a bride, or quasi-oriental ecstasy. Its word-consciousness, its mind's weather—all remains Hesperian. As its verses move toward an image of southerly flight (the poem's nearest analogue to transcendence), patterns emerge that delay the poet's "transport to summer." Perception dwells on the border and refuses to overdefine. So "fullgrown lambs" rather than "sheep." Add such verbal ponderings or reversing repetitions as "borne aloft . . . hilly bourn," a casual chiasmic construction, playing on a mix of semantic and phonetic properties. Or the noun-adjective phrase "treble soft" which becomes an adjective-noun phrase when "treble" is resolved into the northern "triple." And consider the northernisms. The proportion of northern words increases perceptibly as if to pull the poem back from its southerly orientation. There is hardly a romance language phrase: sound-shapes like sallows, swallows, borne, bourn, crickets, croft, predominate. And, finally, the poise of the stanza's ending, on the verge of flight like joy always bidding adieu. How easily, in comparison, Hölderlin turns eastward, and converts wish into visionary transport on the wings of an older rhetoric:

> These my words, when, rapt
> faster than I could have known,
> and far, to where I never
> thought to come, a Genius
> took me from my own house. They glimmered
> in the twilight, as I went,
> the shadowy wood
> and the yearning brooks
> of my country; I knew the fields no more;
> Yet soon, brighter and fresher,
> mysterious
> under the golden smoke
> flowering, rising fast before me
> in the sun's steps
> with a thousand fragrant hills
> Asia dawned.
>
> ("Patmos")

Less magnificent, equally magnanimous, "To Autumn" remains a poem "in the northwind sung." Its progress is merely that of repetitions "in a finer tone," of "widening speculation," of "treble soft" surmise. Yet in its Hesperian reach it does not give up but joins a south to itself.

Keats's respect for the sublime poem does not have to be argued. There is his irritation with the "egotistical sublime" of Wordsworth, his admiration for Milton who broke through "the clouds which envelope so deliciously the Elysian field of verse, and committed himself to the Extreme," his anguished attempt to write the *Hyperion*, and the testimony of lesser but affecting verses like those to the "God of the Meridian" in which he foresees madness:

> when the soul is fled
> To high above our head,
> Afrighted do we gaze
> After its airy maze,

> As doth a mother wild,
> When her young infant child
> Is in eagle's claws—
> And is not this the cause
> Of madness?—God of Song,
> Thou bearest me along
> Through sights I scarce can bear

The "bear . . . bear" pun shows well enough the tension of epic flight. I must now make clear what kind of problem, formal and spiritual, the sublime poem was.

A first difficulty centers on the relation of romance to sublime or epic. The romance mode, for Keats, is now presublime (and so to be "broken through") and now postsublime. Where, as in the first *Hyperion*, Keats wishes to sublimate the sublime he turns with relief to the "golden theme" of Apollo after the Saturnine theme of the first two books. In the *Fall of Hyperion*, however, romance is an Elysium or Pleasure-garden to be transcended. While in "La Belle Dame sans Merci" romance becomes sheer oxymoron, a "golden tongued" nightmare.

It is best to find a view beyond this special dialectic of romance and epic in Keats, all the more so as that is complicated by the dream-truth, or vision-reality split. No formal analysis will disentangle these rich contraries. It can only reduce them to the difference suggested in the *Fall of Hyperion* between "an immortal's sphered words" and the mother-tongue. This is the dichotomy on which Keats's epic voyage foundered: the opposition between Miltonic art-diction and the vernacular. "Life to him [Milton] would be death to me." "English must be kept up." Yet such a distinction is no more satisfying than one in terms of genre. Vernacular romance is perhaps more feasible than vernacular epic—but we get as mixed up as Keats himself when we define each genre in family terms and put romance under mother, epic under father. In the *Fall of Hyperion* Moneta is as patriarchal as she is womanly.

A solution is to consider both romance and epic—or the high-visionary style in general—as belonging to an older, "epiphanic" structuring of consciousness. Against it can be put a nonepiphanic structuring; and if the older type is primarily associated with the East, the modern would be with the West or, at its broadest, Hesperia. It is possible to treat this distinction formally as one between two types of structuring rather than two types of consciousness. Eventually, however, Keats's charge of superstition or obsolescence against the earlier mode will move us into ideology and beyond formalism. A man who says, like Keats, that life to Milton is death to him is concerned with more than formal options.

Epiphanic structure implies, first of all, the possibility of categorical shifts: of crossing into *allo genere*, and even, I suppose, out of ordinary human consciousness into something else. Apotheosis (as at the end of *Hyperion*), metamorphosis, and transformation scenes are type instances of such a crossing. It is accompanied by a doctrine of states, a philosophy of transcendence, and a formulary for the "translation" of states. Epiphanic structure can bear as much sophisitication as an author is capable of. Take the sequence, based on *Paradise Lost*, book 8, which haunted Keats: "The Imagination may be compared to Adam's Dream: He awoke and found it truth." This refers chiefly to Adam seeing Eve first in dream and, upon waking, in the flesh. Keats will often use it ironically rather than not use it at all. So in the "Eve of St. Agnes" Madeline wakes into Imagination's truth and finds it—how pale, how diminished! She melts the reality— Porphyro—back into her dream in a moment of, presumably, sexual union.

A more complex instance is the dark epiphany in "La Belle Dame sans Merci" where the enchanted knight wakes, as it were, into the arms of the wrong dream and cannot find his way back to the right one. Whereas, in Milton, one cunning enjambment expresses the intensity of the quest springing from imaginative loss,

> She [Eve] disappear'd, and left me dark, I wak'd
> To find her

a moment Keats repeats faintly in the Autumn ode,

> Sometimes whoever seeks abroad may find
> Thee

in "La Belle Dame" there is nothing—no natural food—can satisfy the knight. He starves for his drug, like Keats so often for the heightened consciousness of epiphanic style.

In *Paradise Lost*, Adam's dream prepares him for the truth he is to meet. Truth is conceived of as a fuller, perhaps more difficult, dream; and God seeks to strengthen Adam's visionary powers by engaging him in these dream-corridors. Instead of a single dramatic or traumatic change there is to be a gradual tempering of the mind. This modification of epiphanic structure may have inspired a favorite speculation of Keats, that happiness on earth would be enjoyed hereafter "repeated in a finer tone and so repeated." Miltonic tenderness, by allowing Adam's consciousness to develop, by giving it time for growth, lightens the all-or-nothing (sometimes, all-and-nothing) character of epiphanic vision. Though the end remains transport and deification, the means are based, at least in part, on a respect for natural process.

The naturalization of epiphanic form is less effective in "La Belle Dame" than in this prototypal sequence from Milton. The reason lies perhaps in the genre as much as in Keats himself. Quest-romance is a particularly resistant example of epiphanic form. Though Spenser helps to detumesce it he also throws its archaic lineaments into relief: his faerie remains a montage, a learned if light superposition. The dominant feature of quest-romance (as of fairy tale) is the ever-present danger of trespass: of stepping all at once or unconsciously into a daemonic field of force. Often the quest is motivated by redeeming such a prior trespass; but even when it starts unburdened it cannot gain its diviner end without the danger of *allo genere* crossings. Keats's knight steps ritually, if unknowingly, into demonry. So also Coleridge's mariner, whose act of trespass is clear but who before it and after crosses also invisible demarcations. From this perspective the exile of Adam and Eve and the wanderings of Odysseus are both the result of a trespass against the divine, or of stepping willy-nilly into a daemonic sphere.

This is not the place to work out the formal variations of quest-romance. But when a poet does succeed in subduing the form, the result is both remarkable and mistakable. In "Strange Fits of Passion" Wordsworth's rider is a becalmed knight from romance whose rhythm parodies the chivalric gallop and who is always approaching yet never crossing a fatal border. The moon that drops and deflates the dreaming into a mortal thought is a pale metonymy of itself when considered against the backdrop of epiphanic romance. It alone belongs to the sphere of "strange fits"; and while it still divides before and after and even suggests that an imaginative or unconscious trespass has occurred, it cannot be drawn fully into the lunatic symbolism of romance. Keats, I think, did not manage to humanize this form: he feared too much that leaving romance behind meant being exiled from great poetry. He was unable to "translate" the inherited code either into the Miltonic Extreme or into Wordsworth's fulfillment of Miltonic tenderness.

And yet: did he not humanize epiphanic form in the special case of the ode? Recent scholarship by Kurt Schlüter and others has established the basic form of the ancient cult-hymn as it impinged on European poetry. The easiest division of the form is, as you might expect, into three: invocation, narrative or mythic portion, and renewed invocation. Sappho's "Ode to Aphrodite" is a clear example, so is Shelley's "Ode to the West

Wind." Basically, however, the structure consists simply of a series of apostrophes or turns petitioning an absent god or attesting his presence. To the modern reader it may all seem somewhat hysterical: a succession of cries modulated by narrative or reflective interludes.

The sublime or greater or Pindaric ode flourished in the eighteenth century like a turgid weed, all pseudo-epiphany and point, bloat and prickles, feeding off an obsolescent style. Dr. Johnson vilified Gray's Pindaric experiments as "cucumbers." The best that can be said for the genre is that like contemporary opera it became a refuge for visionary themes: an exotic and irrational entertainment which reminded the indulgent consumer of the polite good sense of his society, and sent him back, all afflatus spent, to trifle with the lesser ode. It is not till Collins that a dialogue begins within the genre between its sublime origins and the English ground to which it is transplanted.

A brief notice of this dialogue in Collins's "Ode to Evening" prepares us for Keats. Collins uses all the features characterizing the sublime ode except one. His extended apostrophe suggests the hieratic distance between votary and the invoked power, anticipates at the same time its presence, and leads into a narrative second half describing in greater detail the coming of the divinity and its effect on the poet. This is followed by a renewed invocation which acts as the poem's coda. The one feature conspicuously absent is the epiphany proper. The invoked personification, evening, is a transitional state, a season of the day, whose advent is its presence. By addressing in epiphanic terms a subject intrinsically nonepiphanic, and adjusting his style subtly to it, Collins opens the way to a new, if still uneasy, nature-poetry.

What adjustments of style are there? The movement of the ode is highly mimetic, as Collins, suiting his numbers to the nature of evening, slows and draws out his musings.

> If aught of oaten stop, or pastoral song,
> May hope, chaste Eve, to soothe thy modest ear,
> Like thy own solemn springs
> Thy springs and dying gales
> O nymph reserved, while now.

Instead of hastening some eclipsing power, or leaping into a fuller present, his verse becomes a programmatic accompaniment to the gradual fall of night. The form, in other words, is self-fulfilling: as the processional verse blends with processional nature, and an expanding shadow (a "gradual, dusky veil") is all of relevation there is, the poet's prayer results in what it asks for: "Now teach me, *Maid* compos'd / To breathe some soften'd Strain." This "now" is only in echo that of an ecstatic, annihilative present: it refers to an actual time of day, and perhaps to a belated cultural moment. With this drawn-out "now" nature-poetry is born:

> and now with treble soft
> The red-breast whistles from the garden-croft;
> And gathering swallows twitter in the skies.

Collins's "soften'd strain," his conversion of epiphanic style, will find its culminating instance in Keats's poetry of process.

That Collins represents Evening as a god is more than a naturalized archaism. Evening, invoked as the source of a new music, stands for Hesperia, the evening-star land; and what the poet asks for, in these prelusive strains, is a genuinely western verse, an *Abendlandpoesie*. Like Keats's Psyche, Evening is a new goddess: the poetic pantheon of the East contained only Sun and Night, but Evening is peculiar to the western hemisphere. In the courts of the East, as Coleridge noted in his *Ancient Mariner*, "At one stride comes the dark." The East, in its sudden dawn and sudden darkness, is epiphanic country. But the English climate, in weather or weather of the mind, has a more temperate, even, evening effect. Collins embraces the idea that his native country, or the cultural region to which it belonged, has a style and vision of its own. He shows spirit of place as a felt influence, and Gothic eeriness as eariness. That is, he uncovers a new sense for nature by uncovering a new sense: the natural ear. What the sublime ode had attempted by overwhelming the eye— or the "descriptive and allegoric style" which dominates the age —Collins achieves through this finer sense. The eye, as in Wordsworth's "Tintern Abbey," and in the last stanza of "To Autumn," is made quiet by "the power of harmony."

In the "Ode to Evening" the concept of a Hesperian poetry conditions even sensory mimesis or impels it into a new region. It is no accident that the last stanza of "To Autumn" contains an evening ode in small. That "Evening Ear," which Collins elsewhere attributes to Milton, is, to use a rare Wordsworthian pun, an *organ of vision*: responsive to a particular climate or "spiritual air" (*Endymion*, 4) in which poets feel themselves part of a belated and burdened culture yet find their own relation to the life of things. As the landscape darkens gently, the blind and distant ear notices tones— finer tones—that had escaped a dominant and picture-ridden eye: a weak-eyed bat flits by, curious emblem, and the beetle emerges winding its horn, as if even pastoral had its epic notes. There is still, in Collins, this airy faery which has often dissolved in Keats—who, however, is never very far from it. What matters is that creatures jargon, like "To Autumn" 's parliament of birds; that the sounds are real sounds, a produce of the air; that the heard is not exclusively divine or human; and that within the sheltering dark of the ear other senses emerge: "I cannot see what flowers are at my feet, / Nor what soft incense hangs upon the bough, / But in embalmed darkness guess each sweet." Here absence is presence, though not by way of mystical or epiphanic reversal. In every temperate zone the air is full of noises.

This sensory ideology, if I may call it such, must have affected Keats one early autumn day looking at stubble fields:

> How beautiful the season is now—How fine the Air. A temperate sharpness about it. Really, without joking, chaste weather—Dian skies—I never lik'd stubble fields so much as now—Aye better than the chilly green of the spring. Somehow a stubble plain looks warm—in the same way that some pictures look warm—this struck me so much in my sunday's walk that I composed upon it.

That ideology is in the air is proven by what follows:

> I always somehow associate Chatterton with Autumn. He is the purest writer in the English language. [Chatterton's language is entirely northern.] He has no French idiom, or particles like Chaucer—'tis the genuine English idiom in English words. I have given up Hyperion. . . . English ought to be kept up.

We have already commented on the northernisms in "To Autumn" 's last stanza: even romance language (let alone romance) is gently shunned. Nothing but "home-bred glory."

Can we see the gods die in "To Autumn," the epiphanic forms dissolve, as it were, before our eyes? Autumn is, by tradition, the right season for this dissolution, or dis-illusion.

> Let Phoebus lie in umber harvest

Stevens writes in "Notes toward a Supreme Fiction,"

> Let Phoebus slumber and die in autumn umber
> Phoebus is dead, ephebe.

But, in tradition also, a new god treads on the heels of the old, and loss figures forth a stronger presence. In Hesperian poetry, from Collins to Keats to Stevens, this entire absence/presence vacillation does no more than manure the ground of the poem, its "sensible ecstasy."

Consider the invocation "Season of mists and mellow fruitfulness." The odic O is hardly felt through the verses immediately fill one's mouth with rich labials extended in a kind of chiastic middle between "Season" and "sun." Nothing remains of the cultic distance between votary and personified power: we have instead two such powers, autumn and sun, whose closeness is emphasized, while the moment of hailing or petitioning is replaced by a presumptive question ("Who hath not seen thee") suggesting availability rather than remoteness. The most interesting dissolve, however, comes with the grammatical shift, in the opening line, from mythic-genealogical to descriptive-partitive "of," which effectively diffuses autumn into its attributes. Compare "Season of mists and mellow fruitfulness" with the following apostrophes:

> Thou foster-child of silence and slow time.

Here the poet uses clearly and finely a formula which alludes to the high descent of the apostrophized object. In our next example

> Nymph of the downward smile, and side-long glance

the grammatical form is analogous, but the "of" has moved from genealogical toward partitive. The nymph is eminently characterized by these two attributes: they *are* her in this statuesque moment. The opening of "To the Nile":

> Son of the old moon-mountains African
> Stream of the pyramid and crocodile

actually brings mythic-genealogical and partitive-descriptive together. Against this background we see how beautifully dissolved into the ground of description is the mythical formula of "To Autumn" 's first line.

We do, of course, by what appears to be a regressive technique, meet Autumn personified in the second stanza. If the poem approaches a noon-point of stasis—of arrest or centered revelation—it is here. The emergence of myth serves, however, to ripen the pictorial quality of the poem rather than to evoke astonishment. The emphasis is on self-forgetful relaxation (at most on "forget thyself to marble") not on saturnine fixation. No more than in "To Evening" is nature epiphanic: Keats's Autumn is not a specter but a spirit, one who steals over the landscape, or "amid her store" swellingly imbues it. The poets's mind is not rapt or astonished and so forced back on itself by a sublime apparition.

It is essential, in fact, to note what happens to mind. In the cult hymn the invocation merges with, or is followed by, the god's *comos*: an enumeration of his acts and attributes. But Keats's first stanza becomes simply the filling up of a form, a golden chain of infinitives hovering between prospect and fulfillment, until every syntactical space is loaded and the poet's mind, like the bees', loses itself in the richness. The stanza, in fact, though full, and with its eleven lines, more than full, is not a grammatical whole but a drunk sentence. The poet's mind, one is tempted to say, has entered the imagined picture so thoroughly that when the apostrophe proper is sprung at the opening of stanza 2, and the grammatical looseness corrected, it simultaneously opens a new speculative movement. And when the generative figure of Autumn appears in the second stanza, it is self-harvesting like the poet's own thoughts. The last stanza, then, leaves us in a "luxury of twilight" rather than dropping us into a void where "no birds sing."

The demise of epiphanic forms in "To Autumn" raises a last question: is not the sequential movement of the whole poem inspired by a progressive idea with Enlightenment roots? There seems to be, on the level of sensation, something that parallels the first *Hyperion*'s progress from heavier to lighter, from Hyperion to Apollo, and from fixed burdens to a softer oppression. Several key phrases in Keats's letters suggest an "enlightenment" of this kind. The poet talks of "widening speculation," of "the regular stepping of Imagination toward a Truth," and of easing the "Burden of the Mystery." Magical moments like the fourth stanza of "Ode on a Grecian Urn"

> Who are these coming to the sacrifice?
> To what green altar, O mysterious priest

are surely related to this lightening. Mystery survives, but in a purged, airy, speculative form. The "overwrought" questions of the ode's beginning, which sought to penetrate or fix a symbol-essence, are purified into surmise and evoke a scene of "wide quietness" rather than bacchic enthusiasm.

There is a progress then; but is it toward truth? We know what the conclusion to the Grecian Urn ode suggests. "Beauty is Truth, Truth Beauty" is a chiasmic phrase, as self-rounding as the urn. No ultimate turn or final step toward a truth occurs. Though there are turns in the poem, they are more musical than epiphanic, and the very notion of "the turn" merges with that of the art-object: Keats turns the urn in his imagination until the urn is its turnings. The poet's speculation is circular.

Keats's rondure, his counterprogression, subverts without rejecting the received idea of "enlightenment." Poetry clearly has its own progress, its own lights. Formalistic or art-centered terms have, therefore, a certain propriety. But they cannot suffice for Keats any more than for Wordsworth, who also seeks to ease the "burthen of the mystery" ("Tintern Abbey," 39). Consider the profound difference between these poets, who both believe in a dispersion of older—poetical or religious—superstitions. Such qualities as decorum, impersonality, symbolic adequacy are a function mainly of the concenteredness of "To Autumn": the poem turns around one image like a "leaf-fring'd legend." Though Wordsworth's poems may also have a center of this kind (Lucy's death, a peculiar landscape, a remembered scene), it rarely appears as picturesque symbol or image. Wordsworth's kernels are mysteries: charged spiritual places which confront and confuse a mental traveler who circles their enchanted ground—or who, like a policeman, tries to cordon off the disturbance. This too is an important "enlightenment" form, delimiting a romance apparition or sublime feelings—yet how different from Keats! In Wordsworth the spirit must find its own containmemt, and never quite finds it; those "spots of time" erupt from their hiding-places like the Hebraic God; the structure of his poems expresses various attempts at containment which accrete with difficulty into a personal history ("Tintern Abbey") or an eschatological and cultural one ("Hart-Leap Well"). But Keats's experience is limited from the outset by Greek or picturesque example. What perplexes his imagination is a mysterious picture rather than a mystery.

Keats's formal a priori takes us back to Greece and where, according to Hegel, modern consciousness began. Formal beauty mediates "between the loss of individuality . . . as in Asia, where spiritual and divine are totally subsumed under a natural form, and infinite subjectivity." Greek character is "individuality conditioned by beauty" and in its respect for divine images modern and free, rather than Asiatic and superstitious. "He [the human being] is the womb that conceived them, he the breast that suckled them, he the spiritual to which their grandeur and purity is owing. Thus he feels himself calm in contemplating them, and not only free in himself, but possessing the consciousness of his freedom."

That Hegel's description can fit Keats makes one cautious about the whole enterprise of dividing consciousness into historically localized phases. All the more so as Hölderlin has his own myth of the Hesperian character, which is said to begin when Homer moderates oriental pathos or "fire from heaven." I make no claim for the historical exactness of either Hegel or Hölderlin. Historical speculation and criticism stand, as Professor Wimsatt has observed, in a highly problematic relationship.

Yet there is something like "Hesperian" freedom in "To Autumn," a poem which becomes—in Hegel's words—the womb for the rebirth of an astral or divine image. Such a divine image is certainly there; we should not exaggerate the absence of poetical superstition in Keats. Though his central figure is picturesque its star quality glimmers through.

Much has been written on Autumn's affinities to Demeter or other harvest deities. The divinity, however, that haunts Keats early and late is Apollo: sun-god, god of song, and "fore-seeing god." The difference between Hyperion and Apollo is, in good part, that the former is now doomed to live under "the burden of the mystery." Hyperion cannot dawn any more; he remains darkling. But Apollo in *Hyperion*, even though that poem breaks off and leaves the young god's metamorphosis incomplete—even though he too must shoulder the mystery—should break forth like the sun to "shape his actions" like "a fore-seeing god." In the Autumn ode the major theme of clairvoyance—at once foreseeing and deep-seeing (deep into the heart or maw of life)—is tempered. Yet is it far from absent.

For Autumn's "conspiring" function is comparable to that of the guardian genius, the *natale comes qui temperat astrum* [Horace, *Epistle* 2.2.187]. An idea of poetic or personal destiny enters, in however veiled a form. The poet who writes this ode stands under the pressure of an omen. As summer passes into autumn (season of the year or human season), his dreaming deepens into foresight:

> When I have fears that I may cease to be
> Before my pen has glean'd my teeming brain,
> Before high-piled books, in charact'ry,
> Hold like rich garners the full-ripen'd grain
>
> . . . . . . . . . . . . . . . . .
>
> Herr: es ist Zeit. Der Sommer war sehr gross

In fear of early death, and sensing riches his pen might never glean, Keats evokes a figure of genial harvests. Three times he renews his surmise of fruitfulness, three times he grasps the shadow without self-defeating empathy. Even fruitfulness is not a burden in "To Autumn." This, at last, is true impersonality.

# Identification and Identity: The "Ode to a Nightingale"

## Stuart A. Ende

The "Ode to a Nightingale" portrays an encounter with an ideal that is antithetical to emotional ties. The famous opening of the ode describes not the initial moment of encounter but a time after the encounter has begun. This is an important distinction, because as we read the first line, the poet has *already* lost self to the seeming demands of the other and so is very much in the same predicament as Saturn at the opening of *Hyperion*, or as Clymene, who experiences a "living death" as a consequence of hearing a "blissful golden melody." The bird's song similarly begins to deprive the poet of life—the life of the "heart" and the "sense," for these elements of a relationship are threatened by the poet's transferring his love to that singer in the trees:

> My heart aches, and a drowsy numbness pains
> > My sense, as though of hemlock I had drunk,
> Or emptied some dull opiate to the drains
> > One minute past, and Lethe-wards had sunk.
> 'Tis not through envy of thy happy lot,
> > But being too happy in thine happiness—
> > > That thou, light-wingèd Dryad of the trees,
> > > > In some melodious plot
> > Of beechen green, and shadows numberless,
> > > Singest of summer in full-throated ease.

From *Keats and the Sublime*. © 1976 by Yale University. Yale University Press, 1976.

The poet's "being too happy" in the bird's own happiness is an instance of "the feel" of feeling—though, as is usual in Keatsean encounters, there is a cost to him in the exercise of such empathy. As love for the antithetical other—a love that is self-surrender—increases, the emotional self is diminished. This threatened loss of self is one way in which the nightingale cheats the poet: it cannot be internalized, the way Psyche was, and by maintaining its remove and demanding the poet's love, it brings about the dangerous feelings of the first two lines. The bird's "ease" is thus ironically recalled in the "easeful Death" the poet invokes later in the poem.

In this context, and with an eye towards Keats's marvelous ability to pun tellingly, the "melodious plot" seems also a "plot" against the poet, an intentional policy of deception. Regardless of these possible threatening elements, however, the poet responds with sympathetic happiness and a delight in the nightingale's ability to sing of the fullness of summer, which is still in the offing. The bird sings of a future fulfillment: the poet, as we learn, cannot "forget" the misery of past and present. The basis of the conflict is, then, largely established in this opening stanza. The nightingale's song has come melodiously to the poet's ear, as the voice of love sounded "melodious" to the Indian Maiden in *Endymion*, and like the sorrowful Maiden the poet is threatened with self-diminution. Keats does not resist, for to do so would be to affirm the egotistical sublime that stands alone. Keats casts out "envy" in favor of a form of negative capability in which he allows the high strains to play upon his sensibility. The soul, as he wrote in his journal letter to the George Keatses, is created by the action of the world on the heart.

At this point, we usually think of the rest of the poem as a successful attempt to join the nightingale, followed by the poet's inevitable separation from it. I myself find that joining ambiguous, and in any case I think there is a more important motive that develops from the encounter: the poet is "caught" by the song at the outset, but as the poem progresses he affirms not the antithetical but the emotional, not the music of heaven but the poetry of earth. An extraordinary generosity may be glimpsed in the poem, as the poet sacrifices self to otherness in what increasingly looks like an attempt to humanize that otherness, by providing it with an emotional context it in itself lacks. In the "Ode to a Nightingale" we begin to reach a more balanced relationship between poet and muse, in which the poet gives even as he begins to understand that the bird does not, except by its presence.

The second stanza invokes wine as a means of reaching the bird and leaving the world "unseen" in its company. That attempt, as readers know, is unsuccessful: it is not until the fourth stanza that the poet learns that the "viewless wings of Poesy," by a sort of fiat, are the only way to the nightingale. It does not seem, however, as if the second stanza—there are only eight in the poem—could be devoted to a mere error of approach. Rather, the wine that the speaker turns to represents an antithesis to the bird—he is even at this point momentarily drawing back from it, in an affirmation of the values that he will later affirm. There is nothing that suggests ecstasy in the wine, which might indeed advance the poet's cause, if this were merely to achieve union with a sublime other. This is a "vintage," as the poet refers to it, that tastes "Of Flora and the country green," and "that hath been / Cooled a long age in the deep-delvèd earth." That is, this is the wine of romance (Flora) rather than the sublime, and if sacramental at all it is so of the earth, not the sky. "Deep-delvèd" suggests the cultivation of the soil, and the cellars used for aging Keats's favorite wine, claret. But it suggests too the ritual of burial, of continual burials and of generations gone before, all of them into that earthly resting place. As such, the image anticipates both the "valley-glades" in which the bird's song is "buried deep" at the end of the poem, and the later toast to mortality that the poet makes in *The Fall of Hyperion*. And it implies an alternative sphere to that of the nightingale, whose presence is necessary to make the ground enchanted, but who has never been part of the human story, of the pathos that Keats has chosen as a necessary basis for imaginative speculation. The second stanza, then, at the same time that it searches for access to the nightingale, delights in the earthly pleasures of wine and romance, and a sensual bliss of which the bird is not a part:

> Oh, for a beaker full of the warm South,
>     Full of the true, the blushful Hippocrene,
>         With beaded bubbles winking at the brim,
>             And purple-stainèd mouth,
> That I might drink, and leave the world unseen,
>     And with thee fade away into the forest dim.

The poet, in a way, is still sparring, in a somewhat Hamlet-like fashion: he has been summoned and has pledged a portion of his allegiance, but he has yet to expose himself to the pain of transition.

The problem is that to join the bird is indeed to "leave the world unseen"—in the double sense, perhaps, of not seeing it as well as not being seen—and so to lose the portraiture intense that remembrance stores. Yet Keats has already ascertained (in earlier poems) the impossibility of recalling romance. He must, them, join the bird, though retain self in doing so.

This dilemma informs the third stanza, which describes the close correlation between "forgetting" human existence and murdering the self that remembers:

> Fade far away, dissolve, and quite forget
> What thou among the leaves hast never known.

The nightingale sings in the dim forest. But to know suffering is also to dim the eyes, though in a contrary way. The "Here" that is earth is a place

> Where but to think is to be full of sorrow
> And leaden-eyed despairs;
> Where Beauty cannot keep her lustrous eyes,
> Or new Love pine at them beyond to-morrow.

The sorrow of thought—which Gray believes destroys paradise—both dims the luster of the eyes and freezes them in despair. This is the burden of pathos, which sees and knows only fleetingness: all its knowledge is that joy is gone. Where in "Ode to Psyche" Keats replaced literal pines with thought, he here finds even emotional pining of brief duration. "As / The physical pine, the metaphysical pine," as Stevens writes in "Credences of Summer."

The graphic despair of the stanza almost seems a necessary prelude to the declaration by which the poet finally launches himself into the vicinity of the nightingale. The reminders of palsy and the premature death of youth evoke a reflexive desire to leave that world. "Away! away!" the poet calls to the bird and vows to join it despite the tendency of the mind to find ambivalence in experience—"Though the dull brain perplexes and retards." The wings of Poesy carry the poet to the region of bird and moon, who perhaps ("haply") overlooks this sacrificial loss of the world from her throne in the night sky:

> Already with thee! Tender is the night,
> And haply the Queen-Moon is on her throne,
> Clustered around by all her starry fays;
> But here there is no light.

" 'Twas to live," Endymion found when he submitted to otherness. That quality of reward is present in these lines as well, though it is as much a reward that the poet bestows as receives. From the outset he softens the darkness: "Tender is the night" is already the beginning of oxymoron, of an antiphonal music of which the nightingale's is only one strain. We note that even the presence of the moon is a surmise, for there is no light "here" where the poet is. Whether the poet is indeed "with" the bird is therefore somewhat debatable. In the next stanza we discover him in the forest, yes, but with his feet on the ground. And if the bird is meant to bring him to the saving light of the moon—Cynthia enthroned—is clearly fails to do so.

With the light gone and the light of visual sense gone out, Keats, in one of his most magnificent passages, nevertheless suspends irritable reaching out in favor of allowing the burden of the mystery to assert itself. The result is a mingling of presence and absence that is unmatched, for the flowers that grow in this landscape recall but are different from those that fill the forests of romance:

> I cannot see what flowers are at my feet,
>> Nor what soft incense hangs upon the boughs,
> But in embalmèd darkness, guess each sweet
>> Wherewith the seasonable month endows
> The grass, the thicket, and the fruit-tree wild—
>> White hawthorn, and the pastoral eglantine;
>>> Fast-fading violets covered up in leaves.

The poet, necessarily, cannot see; but his dark grows luminous and fruitful. Keats is remembering the flowers of *A Midsummer Night's Dream* (2.1.249–52) and perhaps also those of "Lycidas" (142–48), but those flowers survive mortality: when Edward King is gone they adopt their "sad embroidery," but the landscapes of both works exist out of time. Keats's flowers know death, know mutability, and never grew in any other landscape.

Thus there are echoes here of other poets and other poems, but the stanza could have been written only by Keats. Wordsworth, in also taking up the burden of the mystery, looked downward to "The Pansy at my feet" (The Intimations Ode, 1.54). Keats again refuses to name, at the outset, though knowledge comes: "I cannot see what flowers are at my feet." This is mortal enchantment, a fire that is only earthly, yet it arises from two elements, each equally necessary. With the flowers, Keats summons, as it were, his ghostly poetic fathers—Shakespeare, Milton, Wordsworth. Their pastoral was his original poetic region and recurs in the early poems in 1817. That summons is made inevitable by the presence of the nightingale, the reminder of Milton, especially: this is the positive side of poetic influence, for fatheral (or parental) presence is necessary to the sublime of the sublime pathetic, to negative capability, as well as to the earlier sublime ode. The second element is the combination of self-acceptance and love, or inner and outer sympathy, that allows the flowers their mortality. There is no hint of "envy," no renunciation that would idealize the flowers and thereby freeze them into permanence. There is only the fullest and most compelling negative capability. The poet is neither the nightingale nor the Queen-Moon, but whereas Hyperion lamented that "I cannot see—but darkness, death and darkness," Keats here finds an "embalmèd darkness," an oxymoron that suggests both death and rich distilled perfume, of his own making. For this simultaneous concession and victory, in which he surrenders to his poetic fathers and yet retains his own feelingful vision, the poet is rewarded with a possible future, in which he, as poetic "child," comes into his own identity and appropriates to himself a "wine" that is not an old romance, and a "summer" that is his and not the nightingale's:

> And mid-May's eldest child,
> The coming must-rose, full of dewy wine,
> The murmurous haunt of flies on summer eves.

If, as Freud came to believe, "character" is a precipitate of lost objects, each of which leaves its shadow on the ego, then this vision is the furthest reach of what it means to live in a world where men grow spectre-thin and die, and even "new" Love flickers in the coming darkness. The poet, who is so powerfully drawn to pathetic representations, forgives their transience as well as his own, and by this gives the darkness its various perfumes. This capability in Keats is not unique to him, but it is extraordinary and touches the other odes as well. The poet has learned Psyche's "secrets" and knows that beautiful things are not joys forever, and that the power of otherness, which instills a fear for sight and for life, cannot be resisted. Yet his feeling for vulnerable objects is so intense as to almost redeem them, usually by means of an adjective that implies both that vulnerability and sympathy—as in these lines from the "Ode on a Grecian Urn":

> Who are these coming to the sacrifice?
> To what green altar, O mysterious priest,
> Lead'st thou that heifer lowing at the skies,
> And all her silken flanks with garlands dressed?
> What little town by river or sea shore,
> Or mountain-built with peaceful citadel,
> Is emptied of this folk, this pious morn?
> And, little town, thy streets for evermore
> Will silent be; and not a soul to tell
> Why thou art desolate can e'er return.

"Little town": it is this recognition that terminates Keats's empathic involvement in the life of the Grecian urn. The poet cannot heal the desolation of the town any more than he can return Orpheus to Calliope or Posthumus to Imogen. But he gives it the gift of feeling, a modicum of recompense for its fall into silence. The "sacrifice," presided over by a "priest" of the mystery, has a quality of inevitability and seems involuntary. The heifer, the town, and perhaps the poet are caught in that mystery and that sacrifice and receive redemption only from the poet. I find the same fair attitude at work in the ode "To Autumn," in which the fiction that "Warm days will never cease" is maintained despite the poet's awareness of a conspiracy behind the fiction. They are still "Warm" days, and to give them this beneficent adjective is to obviate both a fearful sublime and a static pathos.

That poetic surrender is partly a wished-for surrender to death is an inescapable conclusion. But to resist this is to deny the human beauty of the catalogue of flowers that die and the paradoxical strength the poet assumes in the face of an antithetical other that was never a part of death yet is involved in the poet's submission to it. As the bird continues to sing, the poet's listening regard begins to assume a deathly quietude, and the nightingale itself emerges as the poetic father, Milton's "wakeful Bird" that "Sings darkling":

> Darkling, I listen; and, for many a time
>   I have been half in love with easeful Death,
> Called him soft names in many a musèd rhyme,
>   To take into the air my quiet breath;
> Now more than ever seems it rich to die,
>   To cease upon the midnight with no pain,
>     While thou art pouring forth thy soul abroad
>       In such an ecstasy!

If the presence of the spectral other overwhelms the poet—enough so that he can envison a death without "pain," without contraries—it does so only as a result of his own softening love. I do not think we can separate death from otherness here: when Keats retrospectively states that he "Called him soft names in many a musèd rhyme," one cannot help seeing the muse in "musèd." Rhymes to the muse bring about addresses to death. To that muse and to that death, Keats surrenders a portion of self (he is only "half in love," after all), but he does so in a humanizing gesture that makes death not an object of terror but something "easeful." That word, curiously, takes us back to "Sleep and Poetry" and "L'Allegro," but rather than the "heart-easing things" of those poems, which did not involve a penseroso strain, the poet juxtaposes his *emotional* tie to the thought of death the nightingale instills, and so mitigates that daemonic threat.

I earlier mentioned the ambiguity of the poet's union with the night-ingale: do we not rather see a dialogue of a kind, in which the "fatheral" nightingale summons the poet to an otherwhere or otherwise (the fairy stealing mid-May's eldest child, as it were), while the poet affirms that his proper place is his English ground, the region of mortal beauty? "Life to him," Keats wrote of Milton (to the George Keatses on September 21, 1819), "would be death to me": "Chatterton's language is entirely north-ern—I prefer the native music of it to Milton's cut by feet I have but lately stood on my guard against Milton. Life to him would be death to me." The dialogue is more inclusive than one between the language of Chatterton and that of Milton. Keats, since the fourth book of *Endymion*, had been seeking the "Muse of my native land," as Chatterton seemed to have found a "native music." This trend reflects a journey homeward to self from the otherness that includes (among other elements) the presence of Milton. It is not clear that there can be a native muse, which in its true form would exclude both otherness and epiphany. But Keats chooses the "here" where there is no light, the darkling region that shadows mortality, which is not the scene of Milton's "Life" but also is not imaginative death to himself. In the encounter with the nightingale, the poet's acceptance of necessary death paradoxically makes him the spokesman for life.

Consequently, when Keats goes on to admire the fact that "Thou wast not born for death, immortal bird," the compliment is also mildly pejorative and serves to distance the nightingale from human experience. The balance between admiration and reservation continues through the presentation of the early history of the song:

> The voice I hear this passing night was heard
> In ancient days by emperor and clown:
> Perhaps the self-same song that found a path
> Through the sad heart of Ruth, when, sick for home,
> She stood in tears amid the alien corn;
> The same that oft-times hath
> Charmed magic casements, opening on the foam
> Of perilous seas in fairy lands forlorn.

The song is eastern, biblical, and finally the song of romance, of the magic portals that frame the perilous visions of fairyland. Its relation to the pathos of Ruth, standing in tears, is wonderfully uncertain. We assume she was consoled by it, but the poet does not quite say so. Can an unchanging ("self-same") song console one who is "sick for home," if this is her native home? Or, from another perspective, can the notion of continuity console those tied to a "passing night"?

The answer to these questions must be yes and no. One hopes this is balance rather than evasion. Keats suggests the negative part in his repetition of the word "forlorn" in the next stanza, in which the inaccessibility of those lands draws the poet away from the nightingale as well. Forlornness, after all, is the later poet's mode rather than the bird's, and once the circumstance of pathos is suggested the separation is begun. (It is also a "native" English word, descended from the Middle English *foreloren*.) So the poet is tolled back to his "sole self," complains about the cheating and deceiving of the fancy (which have been apparent for some time), and bids the nightingale a melancholy farewell:

> Adieu! adieu! Thy plaintive anthem fades
>> Past the near meadows, over the still stream,
>>> Up the hill-side; and now 'tis buried deep
>>> In the next valley-glades:
>> Was it a vision, or a waking dream?
>> Fled is that music . . . Do I wake or sleep?

The "yes" of the answer is apparent when we consider the landscape the bird is leaving: this is the "hill-side" that we associate with vision in Keats, but "the still stream" returns us to Saturn's dismal prospect, in which "A stream went voiceless by." There is a suggestion, then, that the departure of the nightingale disenchants the landscape, and therefore we infer the necessary presence of the other to the poet's song, even if this be in mortal notes. When the poet buries the bird's song, he cannot tell sleep from wakefulness: Milton's nightingale, on the other hand, is the wakeful bird.

# Keats and a New Birth:
## The "Ode on Melancholy"

## Leslie Brisman

*Even the wisest among you is only a disharmony and hybrid of plant and phantom. But do I bid you become phantoms or plants? . . . I conjure you,* my brethren, remain true to the earth, *and believe not those who speak unto you of superearthly hopes!*

—NIETZSCHE, Thus Spake Zarathustra

*To retranslate man back into nature, to master the many vain enthusiastic glosses which have been scribbled and painted over the everlasting text,* homo natura, *so that man might henceforth stand before man as he stands today before that* other *nature, hardened under the discipline of science, with unafraid Oedipus eyes and stopped-up Ulysses ears, deaf to the lures of the old metaphysical bird-catchers who have been fluting in at him all too long that "you are more! You are superior! You are of another origin!"—this may be a strange, mad task, but who could deny that it is a task!*

—NIETZSCHE, Beyond Good and Evil

For the poet concerned about inspiration and about his place in what Keats called "the grand march of intellect," the ordinary march of nature seems to proceed with enviable regularity. Overlooking the nature of human sexuality and generational gaps, one sees "out there," in natural history, that season succeeds season, era succeeds era, without the new having to justify its place and without the old threatening to occupy more than its place. In literary history succession is always problematic, both in terms of the individual poet's progress from one moment of inspiration to another and in terms of continuity from one poet to another. The problems are

From *Romantic Origins*. © 1978 by Cornell University. Cornell University Press, 1978.

accentuated when one's precursor seems to have preempted even the awareness of the difference between natural and intellectual succession.

For Keats, Milton—even more than Wordsworth—was the great orig-
inator of that awareness. Milton wrote the central elegy about experiential
loss and spiritual renewal, and he wrote *the* epic about man falling out with
nature. Most important, he represented in his own person the alienation
from the continuity of nature, lamenting that "with the Year / Seasons
return, but not to me returns / Day" (*Paradise Lost*, 3.40–42). Like Wordsworth, Keats sought a counter to Miltonic discontinuity which would represent inspiration renewed as faithfully as are plants and seasons. The search
for or appeal to such a counter-myth of continuity not only underlies Keats's
greatest work in the odes and *Hyperion* poems but justifies a studied lightness
throughout the poetry—a lightness all his own—under the auspices of which
new bursts of inspiration seem to spring up from the earth. . . .

Naturalization and new birth assume [an ironically] lighthearted form
in "Ode on Melancholy." Canceling an original opening stanza of Gothic
claptrap, Keats retained a subtler balance between one stanza of unnatural
recourses and one stanza of natural origins for Melancholy:

1

No, no, go not to Lethe, neither twist
  Wolf's-bane, tight-rooted, for its poisonous wine;
Nor suffer thy pale forehead to be kiss'd
  By nightshade, ruby grape of Proserpine;
Make not your rosary of yew-berries,
  Nor let the beetle, nor the death-moth be
    Your mournful Psyche, nor the downy owl
A partner in your sorrow's mysteries;
  For shade to shade will come too drowsily,
    And drown the wakeful anguish of the soul.

2

But when the melancholy fit shall fall
  Sudden from heaven like a weeping cloud,
That fosters the droop-headed flowers all,
  And hides the green hill in an April shroud;
Then glut thy sorrow on a morning rose,
  Or on the rainbow of the salt sand-wave,
    Or on the wealth of globed peonies;

> Or if thy mistress some rich anger shows,
>   Emprison her soft hand, and let her rave,
>     And feed deep, deep upon her peerless eyes.

The stanza of natural origins seems as full of lighthearted demystification as its predecessor, and four lines mock while describing the advent of melancholy like a change in season or weather. Referring to an "April shroud" rather than an April shower, Keats show how easily darkness can make its abode in the "viewless winds" of metaphor as well as climate. A formalist could say simply that the idea of an April shroud or deathlike spring is paradoxical, and that paradox is a form of playfulness the siege of contraries can take. The readiness with which such observations can be made accounts for the popularity of Keats among the New Critics when having to choose a Romantic: he "teaches best," granted that awareness of irony or the simultaneous presence of conflicting meanings is a primary stage in the appreciation of poetry.

Beyond static contraries, however, is the temporality of natural process and the potentially antipathetic temporality of verse. Isolating the words expressive of mood in the first four lines of the stanza, we find melancholy, weeping, drooping, and the shroud of death. While the fact of death might be said to explain melancholy, weeping, and drooping, Keats's lines mischievously suppose the anteriority of melancholy; it simply falls and becomes mourning rather than the other (Freudian) way round. The stanza begins in simile: melancholy fits fall like rain; one falling action is compared to another. When we discover not simply "cloud" but "weeping cloud," we meet a poetic equivalent for the anteriority of nature—as though nature knew all about weeping before the poet began looking for things to compare to melancholy fits. Similarly, one comes upon "April shroud" having needed only "April shower," and thus seems to discover the melancholy already there. As the Indian Maid says about Sorrow, "she is so constant and so kind," waiting for us, ready to bestow all we are ready to consume. Hence "glut thy sorrow on a morning rose" (the morning is already mourning; consciousness of ephermerality is caught in the bud) for nature will have anticipated one's appetite for melancholy anyway.

Though one could argue that the presence of an image like "weeping cloud" when we are prepared only for "cloud" points to the anteriority of language (the metaphors seem to have the melancholy before the earth does), language is in fact but figuring the priority of nature. Keats's rhetorical strategy is based on our provisional acceptance of a common synecdoche: if we speak of the earth when we mean nature, then the poet, literalizing "earth," can picture melancholy falling to the earth from a prevenient source in the sky. But no, we say, correcting ourselves, there is no question of temporally distinguishing earth from sky, green hills from clouds, but of distinguishing earthly or natural from supernatural or unnatural sources of melancholy. Thus we come to the earthiness of melancholy with the energy of rejecting a literalism; and, with Antaeus-like strength, we grasp what is, after all, precisely the point: melancholy is of the earth whence joy's grapes grow, and is there not just in the autumn but from the first April shower.

If the poetic desire to invent or discover melancholy is preempted by nature, the desire to personify melancholy is preempted by the appearance of a source of melancholy in facing a natural person. We meet the mistress of stanza two before we encounter the veiled goddess of stanza three. But the question of prevenience is much complicated by the conditional of stanza two ("if thy mistress some rich anger shows") and the discovered eternal presence in stanza three: "Ay, in the very temple of Delight / Veiled Melancholy has [she has had, and she now has] her sovran shrine." To clarify Keats's argument about time, compare this Spenser sonnet, which ends with a figure that looks very much like an "original" in relation to Keats's remarkable variation:

> This holy season, fit to fast and pray,
> Men to devotion ought to be inclynd:
> Therefore, I lykewise, on so holy day,
> For my sweet saynt some service fit will find.
> Her temple fayre is built within my mind,
> In which her glorious ymage placed is,
> On which my thoughts doo day and night attend,
> Lyke sacred priests that never thinke amisse.
> There I to her, as th' author of my blisse,
> Will builde an altar to appease her yre;
> And on the same my hart will sacrifise,
> Burning in flames of pure and chaste desyre:
> The which vouchsafe, O goddesse, to accept,
> Amongst thy deerest relicks to be kept.
>
> (*Amoretti*, 22)

Both Spenser's sonnet and Keats's ode move from a playfully hypothetical situation to a more serious look at a present truth. Spenser begins by setting himself the proposition: if one is going to have to be devotional, let the mood at least take the following form; Keats begins by setting a hypothetical listener the proposition: if one is going to have to be melancholy, let the mood at least take the following source. In the end Spenser moves from the optative to the present tense of apostrophe: "vouchsafe, O goddesse, to accept, / Amongst thy dearest relicks to be kept." In the end Keats moves from the optative through the strong statement of what "is" and what must be to the concluding prophecy: "His soul shall taste the sadness of her might, / And be among her cloudy trophies hung."

The significance of these similarities and differences may be related to Spenser's beginning from the serious perspective of Christian devotion (the Easter season) and coming to apostrophize the new god (the lady, so elevated for the space of this poem). Keats begins with a playful account of the old gods and the old remedies of love (Pluto's lethe, Persephone's nightshade) and comes to divinize Melancholy. In the course of the ode he goes further back than the old devotion (finds a truer source) and goes further than the old mistress-worship to proclaim a prophetic truth of universal experience. If Spenser is a great original for Keats's naturalism, the ephebe must overgo his predecessor at his own game. Spenser's mastery is clearest in the surprising figure. "There I to her, as th' author of my blisse, / Will builde an altar to appease her yre." The "as," at first an indication of likeness, slides out of comparison into causality: since she is author of my bliss (since she, as author, precedes my poetic figurations), she has an anteriority and an autonomy that make her emotional state out of my control; she may well be angry, and need appeasement. This tribute to the extrapoetic lady— bringing with it an acknowledgment of art's limitations—is one of Spenser's most characteristic and most endearing achievements in his poems of courtship and marriage. Keats does not rival Spenser in attributing more "earliness" or more extrapoetic reality to the mistress of stanza two; what he does is to seize on his fiction of an angry mistress and ask that one "feed deep, deep upon her peerless eyes," discovering there, in the energy of that anger, a *source* of animation. By itself the figure of angry eyes is traditional— indeed, it is the central figure of *Amoretti* 21, the immediately preceding Spenser sonnet. Spenser's mistress can "traine and teach me with her looks"; what she teaches is of moral or social worth. What the mistress of Keats's ode teaches is, simultaneously, the need to take pleasure in an expression of energy—be it a street fight or a lover's quarrel—and the need to take sorrow back to the same transient source.

In the "Ode to Psyche," the poet finds that if he is belated at all he is fortunately belated and can create for Psyche as goddess what history has not provided her. In the "Ode on Melancholy," the poet finds he is fortunately belated in a more difficult sense and can create for Melancholy as goddess what nature has already provided him. The "Veil'd Melancholy" of stanza three is preceded by the mistress of peerless eyes, and the injunction to "feed deep, deep upon her peerless eyes" is causal, rather than simply parallel to "taste the sadness of her might." Both statements are set in a context of mock indulgence, making their Tantalus-like offerings with the knowledge that there is no satisfaction in self-satisfaction. The richness of a lady's anger is an object of aesthetic pleasure only to one detached to the point of melancholy. The lady with her fit of anger and the gentleman with his melancholy fit realizing he feeds alone on the beauty of her eyes—they are having separate fits. Grounded in nature, knowledge of this separation becomes emblemized by the veil of Melancholy that separates her from those discovering her might. The emblem not only transcends but eases the condition of nature. Better one's soul should be the trophy of the unapproachable than the trifle of the reproaching lady. To be sure, a natural lady's anger passes, and that whole image is playfully presented as a source of melancholy. But whatever the degree of woe or play, the relationship between the natural mistress and the mythologized Melancholy is not a parallelism but a redemptive begetting of the mythic from the natural.

If one considers other literary sources as having a hand in the begetting of the final stanza, a similar but richer argument develops about the priority of nature and her spokesman, Keats. Douglas Bush sites *Troilus and Cressida*:

> What will it be
> When that wat'ry palates taste indeed
> Love's thrice-repured nectar? Death, I fear me;
> Sounding destruction; or some joy too fine,
> Too subtile-potent, tun'd too sharp in sweetness
> For the capacity of my ruder powers.

Speaking these lines, Troilus anxiously anticipates the sorrows of love. The speaker of Keats's ode, in advising a hypothesized seeker after Melancholy to "burst joy's grape against his palate fine," approaches him from the perspective of Shakespeare's play, from presumed familiarity with the ways of love. Thus a source of anxiety for Troilus becomes a source of authority for Keats the speaker of this poem, secure in his knowledge of what poetry has come before him.

If we reach further back in literary history, Theocritus's twenty-third idyll offers a more extended though weaker precursor text, and one Keats could be said transumptively to surpass. Though Theocritus is early this idyll is a late, corrupt, pseudo-Theocritus text in which a lover sets about doing just what Keats's ode argues against. Keats's opening line, "No, no, go not to Lethe," could be a response to Theocritus's lover, who announces that he will take the path to Lethe, "where, men say, is the common cure for lovers' ills-oblivion. Yet if I set it to my lips and drain it to the dregs, not even so shall I quench my longing. And now at last I find pleasure at thy door. I know what is to be. Fair is the rose also, yet time withers it." Keats's advice, "glut thy sorrow on a morning rose," comes like an antithetical response. Theocritus's lover is excluded by the indifference and the anger of the boy with whom he has fallen in love; Keats's lover is advised to feed on anger and by anticipatory knowledge to gain some victory over the evanescence of passion. The poems as a whole are as distinguished as their lovers in their relationship to loss: while Theocritus's idyll is overtaken by its melodramatic conclusion, Keats's poem sets out to find melancholy, and so seems the earlier, less corrupt text. Assurance in "Theocritus ("I know what is to be") is purchased at the price of the conjunction of the death of passion (roses and beautiful boys both fade) with the death of the speaker, which he takes upon himself. A greater assurance is achieved in Keats by preempting the mortality of passion for the passion of anger in stanza two—which seems, for a moment, to leave alive the passion of love—and then substituting in stanza three the sure knowledge of evanescence. Finally, Theocritus's lover literally hangs himself in the doorway of the beloved, while Keats's hypothesized lover will find himself hung (a greater reduction than "hanged"? or a metaphoric and therefore easier one?) mid the trophies in the temple of delight. Never penetrating the temple, Theocritus's lover is left at the door, gaining in death a priority over the death of desire as crude as *ejaculatio praecox*. If Keats's lover needed to wait for acceptance and consummation to achieve his melancholy death, he would indeed be belated. But the absurdity of this extension to Theocritus's literalism brings us round to the achieved priority of the ode: even if melancholy can only be "seen" and "tasted" by the experiential lover, it can be sufficiently known by one who knows what the ode knows about melancholy. As a piece of advice the third stanza of the ode seems to argue ambiguously "know this!" or "you need to experience this!" A psychoanalytic reading might find Keats granting poetic priority to the first over the second of these alternatives as a way of countering the priority of biographical fact—lack of sexual experience. But the poem is stronger, and argues that either injunction restores the would-be lover and the poet with him to the original mutability of sexuality in nature as well as human relations, and makes a text like Theocritus's idyll seem belated and in more than one sense corrupt.

# Voice in the Leaves:
## The "Ode on a Grecian Urn"

*Paul H. Fry*

In an important essay, Helen Vendler has argued that Keats's odes are best understood if we try to locate their "experiential beginnings," by which she means, not necessarily that we should study his biography, but that we should look for points of special intensity in the odes themselves, around which each poem will then appear to take shape. At such points a veil seems to fall away, and the poet confronts, without further evasion, some inescapable force of existence. We should not assume, Vendler says, that the motive of a Keatsian ode appears at the beginning of the text; rather it is worked toward and then in some degree resolved or placated. In my opinion these observations perfectly account for the course of the "Ode to a Nightingale," which is indeed, as Vendler almost alone has argued, a poem that concerns the awareness of death itself as an experiential beginning. Whatever the beauties of the first stanzas in "Nightingale," they are still postponements of an awareness that begins when the poet confesses his wish to die. I turn somewhat from Vendler's essay only when she maintains that the "Ode on a Grecian Urn" has a new and separate experiential beginning. "Grecian Urn" as I read it takes up and continues the subject that was uncovered in "Nightingale": the dialectical debate between death sublimated in art (immortality achieved through imaginative power) and living in the world with death (presence to Being achieved through the genius of camouflage).

This subject plays itself out in "Grecian Urn," leading however toward

---

From *The Poet's Calling in the English Ode.* © 1980 by Yale University. Yale University Press, 1980.

a strange conclusion, so wholly distinct in mode and mood from what precedes it that we never quite decided how to read it. My own choice is to read the ode in a way that will make the ending seem plausible as a retrospective irony. This viewpoint can only be arrived at gradually, but it is well to begin by pointing out that the ending unquestionably harbors a *generic* irony. Whatever we make of its meaning, the final "point" of Keats's ode is exactly appropriate for the generic tradition to which its identity as an "Ode on" is joined. This ode is an inscription or epigram, and should be envisioned as though it were inscribed on a described object; the irony in Keats's case is that his concluding homily, which Lessing characterized for epigrams in general as an *Aufschluss* or extracted message, is the only part of the poem that we can possibly imagine *not* to be extracted; this is, to be inscribed literally on the urn. As an epigram, then, "Grecian Urn" concludes with an irony of presentation that returns us to its equally strong identity as an "ode to": if what is inscribed is abstracted or secondary, and certainly unclear, what is evoked or called forth in the body of the poem is the vivid rendering of the surface of a thing; far more than the inscription, the evocation is "realized" in the relatively strict sense of that term. More ode than epigram because it is more associative than inscriptive, "Grecian Urn" is, then, what Leo Spitzer has authoritatively called it, a *Dinggedicht*—or, to render the term in English with its proper ambiguity, a "poem on a thing."

I shall not be concerned as much with the ontology of the poem, which, again, I think it shares with "Nightingale," as with a related aesthetic topic, namely, the superiority of a certain sort of lyric to the plastic arts and to other sorts of (verbal or nonverbal) "melodies." Keats's Dinggedicht is a poem that supplements a thing; at one and the same time it distances the thing and opens it outward by removing it from space and projecting it into the softer boundaries of time. In entering time, the "leaf-fring'd legend" of the urn begins to flourish and change.

The "Ode on a Grecian Urn" is a hermeneutic lyric that offers itself by way of example as a theory of interpretation. In so doing, it deforms itself, as we shall see, and becomes Keats's version of the unstructuring daemon in a presentational ode. Keats's ode is an attack on the notion that form constitutes a value in and of itself, and thus it reveals a new facet of his odes' continuous theme, the contrast between shapeless genius and shaping power. In itself the urn is a figure of power that immortalizes the dead, like the abstracted nightingale. In the Nightingale Ode, the bird had become an art object when it was transformed into an "immortal bird," and from that moment on the earlier ode, like "Grecian Urn," was about "art and life." A more subtle distinction between the two poems is needed than the one usually alleged between nature invoked and art invoked. Both poems concern art, but not the same kind of art; if the Nightingale Ode is a critique of all poetic genres but its own, "Grecian Urn" broadens the critique to include not only the alien genres but the plastic arts. It pronounces all art that is palpable, visible, or melodic to be trapped in its medium and cut off from any realm of signification beyond itself until it is supplied with the sort of hermeneutic commentary that appears in an ode.

"What leaf-fring'd legend haunts about thy shape?" Like Psyche, knowledge of sources is a haunting intuition beyond shape, yet it can only arise in the vicinity of something that has a shape. If a poem is to capture any of that intuition, it should never come full circle. It should be left open, and accordingly, Keats's fourth stanza leaves the surface of the urn. Meanwhile, though, he experiments with *ecphrasis*, the doctrine of containment by form, and tries by means of dialectic to imitate the rondure of the urn. Not to prejudice the reader against the rather mechanical coldness of the ecphrastic ideal, the experiment begins with the most human metaphor for a circle that exists; the circle of art is addressed as if it were the family circle of man:

> Thou still unravish'd bride of quietness,
>   Thou foster-child of silence and slow time,
> Sylvan historian, who canst thus express
>   A flowery tale more sweetly than our rhyme

Since these lines fully anticipate the course of dispute in the poem, they may usefully detain us. The urn is a family, perhaps a holy family: an unravished bride must have a foster child if she is to be a mother, and the paternal historian need not therefore be named as the father. Through the slippage of apposition, the urn makes these relationships less generative by becoming, in turn, each member of the family itself; that is, as a figure of art, it represents empathy, the entering of others that is not sexual. Thus the urn is a human totality that has been bred in purity. Of course, it has been necessary to deform this passage in order to read it this way, and that necessity is itself significant. An ode that celebrates totality should surely invoke figures that can enter formal relations without hindrance, yet the holistic reading of this passage is in effect an antithetical one, while the disturbances of the holistic reading belong to the drift of the overt argument. In point of fact, as every reader knows, the exact sense of these first lines is extremely evasive.

The appearance of a comma after "still" in the text published in *Annals of the Fine Arts* has satisfied many readers that "still" means "quiet," and that the bride therefore has nothing to fear. But apart from the difficulty of reading "quiet bride of quietness," clearly the presence of "slow time" in the next line suggests that the bride cannot be intact forever. Because, being unravished, she can bear no fruit, she can have no contents except the quiet of death. She *is* a quiet bride of quiet, midway between a stillness before and a stillness after: she once contained the ashes that she will herself become. Hence the first line establishes the intimacy of the urn with death; that is the urn's primary condition. The second line, fostered by the first, presents its secondary condition. Both stillness and quietness, we assume, approach timelessness, and thus in the first line the urn is most intimately related to the circumference or framework of time, which is death. By contrast, the urn is related by adoption, in the second line, to time itself. Consciousness in history, cultural consciousness, acts custodially toward the artifacts it adopts as children—acts more conscientiously toward them in fact than toward its true children, the creatures of nature, including man, whom it takes for granted. The first two lines read together, then, harbor a paradox: holistic art is akin to death, it is like a life accomplished or consummated, but is has no kinship with the germinal cycle of the life it is conventionally said to affirm and justify.

The word "silence" in the second line must be supposed to differ from "still" and "quietness" in the first. If "silence and slow time" suggests a second marriage, that marriage too is a fruitless one that must adopt the urn; or if, to read the phrase as a hendiadys, silence is cognate with slow time, then it is like Wordsworth's "still sad music" and looks forward to the "ditties of no tone" in the next stanza. But none of these three terms for the absence of existential noise, whatever the differences between them may be, are intrinsic attributes of the urn itself; they are genetively but not germinally linked with the urn. The resonance of this variously conceived quiet can be heard near the urn, before and after it, but is never a part of it. The silent extremes of intuition and death precede the urn ("still"), and the silent extremes of contemplation and death come after it. In Crocean terms, which are highly relevant to the study of Keats's thought, all the modalities of silence constitute an "intuition-expression," while the work of art that is externalized, made manifest in a concrete medium, is merely a "represented expression." It begins to be apparent that the "Ode on a Grecian Urn" entertains what is perhaps the ultimate irony for an ode; it rejects the heard melodies of voice and prefers the leafage of writing. The lines "*Sylvan* historian, who canst thus express / A flowery tale more sweetly than our rhyme" reveal this preference meatphorically, even though the dialectical plan of the poem will not yet permit the assignment of preferred metaphors to preferred media. Later, the best foliage will lack the flowers of rhetoric.

Since the rest of the stanza poses baffled questions of the sort that history could have answered readily enough, the urn as historian is shown to fail because it offers the past without interpretation. Like the deferential listener of the Nightingale Ode, the museum goer of this ode is guilty of an initial false modesty in pretending that the urn is wiser than he is. While it is not quite true that the urn explains nothing, it is certainly true that its way of communicating offers no instruction. Knowledge belongs rather to the inspiration that precedes expression and the interpretation that succeeds it. The surrounding of the round urn, necessarily but also deliberately kept from touching the urn's expressive surface, is the hermeneutic circle. Interpretation, the unfolding map or "legend" that helps us to read the urn, is an *un*expressive voice because it is indeterminate. It haunts shapes but itself resists being shaped into melody; it is a ditty of no tone, like "The murmurous *haunt* of flies on summer eves," that is rich in inconclusive knowledge. As John Jones remarks, Keats "wants to *write* a Grecian urn." But for the moment, Keats leaves an opening through which his argument can subtly develop by confining the urn's eventually victorious rival, poetry, to the trivial-seeming channel of "rhyme." The pet-lamb versifying (see the "Ode on Indolence") implied by "our rhyme" is the collective enterprise of tame hymnody from which an ode always alienates itself. Here, though, "our rhyme" is left to stand for poetry in general in order to keep our critical attention trained on the urn.

The best gloss on the comparative values I have imputed to Keats's ode was soon to be written by Shelley in the *Defence of Poetry*:

> For language is arbitrarily produced by the imagination, and has relation to thoughts alone; but all other materials, instruments, and conditions of art, have relations among each other, which limit and interpose between conception and expression. The former is as a mirror which reflects, the latter as a cloud which enfeebles, the light of which both are mediums of communication.

It is not just the formal constraint imposed by the plastic and acoustic media, but their derivation from nature, from the world they are meant to represent, that muddles their communication: that is, they stand as an intermediate opacity between referee and referent, as a wall—in the present case a marble wall—that blocks the line of vision. For both Shelley and Keats, in the transvaluation that results from this insight, the Letter is closely associated with what is usually called the Spirit, while the material media have the dry obstinacy that is usually attributed to the Letter.

The questions that Keats asks the urn not only reveal its opacity simply in being questions, but also repeat in content the antimony between the finite and the borderless that is presented everywhere in the poem:

> What leaf-fring'd legend haunts about thy shape
> Of deities or mortals, or of both,
>> In Tempe or the dales of Arcady?
> What men or gods are these?

The ensuing questions vary this theme as an antimony between capture and the failure to capture:

>> What maidens loth?
> What mad pursuit? What struggle to escape?
> What pipes and timbrels? What wild ecstasy?

Here both states, capture and escape, are ambivalently valued, even before their dialectical relation becomes the main subject of the second and third stanzas. Capture, the triumph of form, is an escape from fulfillment and an entrapment of potential. Escape, on the other hand, here imagined as the ecstasy of free-standing, is a failure to encircle or be encircled that restores the intuition of potential.

"What pipes and timbrels?" is understandably taken by a good many readers to be a silly question. It is only in the next stanza that the motive of this question appears. But even then, it still seems strange that with pottery and poetry already on his hands the poet should now take up music, joining his ode briefly to the Pythagorean-Boethian tradition that prefers "theoretical music" to "practical music," and thus sketching the outline of an ode against the Power of Music like Dryden's. Music and poetry are, in fact, as in odes for music, parallel if not identical. Heard melodies are poems of imaginative Power, while ditties of no tone are odes of Genius. Not just the plastic arts and music, now, but also rhetorical poetry, poetry full of flowery tonality but lacking the finer tone, all are equally subject to Keats's critique of form. The "soft pipes," which are *not silent* pipes, hum like the "murmurous haunt" of the sound of being. Keats has accusingly asked "What pipes and timbrels?" because he knows that the urn cannot know the answer. The urn represents absolute silence that is meant to be melodic, whereas the modestly hermeneutic ode "plays" to the inner ear a sound between silence and melody that is infinitely resonant; written among the leaves, it is the toneless potential of all sound.

At this point the first round of argument in behalf of the diminished or attenuated lyric, of an ode that is not like an ode, is complete; and for the next sixteen lines the poet lectures the figures on the urn in the full irony of having just proved that they cannot hear him. His ode now steers its course between the mute and undeclaring figures of silence and the passions of real life, which latter are just as unpoetic as the urn figures because they are not quieted and transmuted by the awareness of Being. The contrast in these lines is not so much between parched longing and *post coitu homo tristis* as between extremes of equally unproductive desire.

That the urn figures are meant to imply one such extreme is rarely disputed, since their "happiness" is quite obviously absurd. The discomfort of their plight is excruciating until we register an irony that is more than an irony; in a burlesque of ecstasy, Keats is imitating the totemistic madness that makes people apostrophize pictures. "Happy" six times: this is a serious joke that echoes the five "nevers" of Lear and the five maudlin "fallens" of Dryden's Timotheus. Perhaps a parody of choral repetition in cantatas and odes for music, this passage is more importantly a parody of Keats's own rather too sentimental portraits of unself-conscious beings in "Psyche" and the Nightingale Ode. The urn figures, then, cannot be envied, being insensate in themselves and acutely frustrated if we humanize them. Once their fair attitude has been interpreted, a contrast between them and "human passion" no longer seems possible:

> All breathing human passion far above,
>     That leaves a heart high-sorrowful and cloy'd,
>     A burning forehead, and a parching tongue.

More than a few passages in the Letters show that by "cloy'd" Keats is not apt to mean "satiated" but rather overburdened and finally numbed, as in "Nightingale," with excess of desire. In other words, neither the urn figures *nor* human lovers can ever "kiss, / Though winning near the goal." All the urn figures, especially the "happy melodist," have the double identity that Keats had first bestowed on the nightingale. Considered apart form the urn, as a "youth, beneath the trees," Keats's piper is no sentimental naif but a voice from the vale of soul-making. But as one who was not born for death, who "cannot leave his song," the youth has a fixed identity that does not belong to the "proud dying" of an ode.

But the song of the musician does set him apart from his speechless companions in desire, whose "parching tongue" makes them incapable of speech, like the Ancient Mariner; in a single phrase, "youth, beneath the trees," Keats marks the intermediary place of a hermeneutic ode between mute figuration and mute desire. Now advancing beyond the surface of the urn, Keats in the fourth stanza demonstrates the strength of an interpretive act that has been released from its bondage to self-enclosed artifacts. For the rondure of a well-wrought urn, Keats now substitutes the moving perspective of an inquisitive eye. Once again the interpreter must ask questions, but now his questions are no longer rhetorical—no longer subservient, that is, to the rhetorical power of the urn. Now his questions are hermeneutic questions to which death alone can provide answers:

> Who are these coming to the sacrifice?
>     To what green altar, O mysterious priest,
> Lead'st thou that heifer lowing at the skies,
>     And all her silken flanks with garlands drest?
> What little town by river or sea shore,
>     Or mountain-built with peaceful citadel,
>         Is emptied of this folk, this pious morn?
> And, little town, thy streets for evermore
>     Will silent be; and not a soul to tell
>         Why thou art desolate, can e'er return.

There are many mysteries in this extraordinary stanza that Keats's legions of interpreters have yet to explore; that is as it should be, for this stanza is Keats's example of the way a "ditty of no tone" should prolong our questioning in becoming a part of it, and not offer its two handles like an amphora to be grasped and emptied by exegesis.

Freed from the single viewpoint that must be taken toward a framed representation, the visionary eye in this landscape roams at will. At the beginning of the stanza the speaker stands in the countryside, watching the townsfolk come toward him, while at the end he is watching, or even within, the silent town. The whole surface of the earth has now become an urn, and the stanza is not "on" but contained within its vast boundaries. The only object that resists being seen is the sacrificial altar itself, though the interpreter can suspect that it is "green." But why green? Altars are not green, unless they appear beneath the leaves, as in "Psyche" with its forest and its inward altar, or as in the "Ode to a Nightingale," with its forest threshold where the humanized piper on the urn still stands in this poem. By leaving the urn, Keats has now more fully entered it, or re-entered it in the Pindaric "*return*" that closes the stanza. Perhaps he is influenced by Wordsworth's sudden discovery of the valley of death where the Solitary lives in *The Excursion*:

> all at once, behold!
> Beneath our feet, a little lowly vale,
> A lowly vale, and yet uplifted high
> Among the mountains; even as if the spot
> Had been from eldest time by wish of theirs
> So placed, to be shut out from all the world!
> Urn-like it was in shape, deep as an urn.
>
> (2.327.33)

Keats's green altar is not located because it is everywhere. It is the sacrificial eye of the poet, landscaped by the poet-priest of "Psyche." The sign or garland of his mystery is the leafy fringe that dresses the sacrificial animal, an unmated "youth" without offspring whose "lowing" is a forlorn sound. Like the mortal nightingale, the heifer stands for all toneless melodists in a state of desire. The little town that is emptied, finally, repeats more poignantly the figures of the urn as a barren family of man that appeared in the first three lines of the poem. The little town is the foster child of acculturation, a defense against mortality that protects only itself, and "shal[l] remain" uninhabited.

The movement toward discovery is ended at this point of "return" to the inspirational locale of all the spring odes. Not just the last two lines but the whole fifth stanza is a "Stand," an *Aufschluss* abstracted to remind us that unlike the hermeneutic eye, with its evocative openness, the urn is merely rhetorical, a "Fair attitude," and, accordingly, barren of knowledge. Because it has a definite "shape," its pictured sides wall out any awareness of Being, and if we take it too seriously it teases us out of interpretation. However noisy and "overwrought" the urn's rhetoric may become, it remains only a "silent form," silent because formal; to repeat, the urn is at once a "heard melody" that leaves nothing to the imagination and a burial of intuition that discloses nothing to the imagination. As an achieved form, the urn proposes itself as an ecphrastic model of "Beauty," and proves the rhetorical nature of its claim by interrupting the poet's interpretation with its own adage. "Beauty is truth, truth beauty" is a variant on the first line of *Endymion*. We may suppose that for many reasons—its jingle, its prematurely palpable design—that line had become an embarrassment for Keats to remember, especially because he had noticed, in the "Ode to a Nightingale," that "Beauty cannot keep her lustrous eyes." The last lines of the "Ode on a Grecian Urn" seem to me to be unequivocally ironic. The urn is the optimistic poet of *Endymion*, the poet who did not know as yet that death is the mother of beauty, and who therefore proclaimed: "A thing of beauty is a joy forever."

The ambiguity of the last two lines is deliberate, and cannot be resolved with certainty; but not as much depends on establishing a preferred reading as is usually thought, since both readings are equally ironic. The urn can tell us that "that" is all we need to know because it is an urn of decidedly limited insight. But we can also tell the urn that "that" is all *it* needs to know; an urn, after all, could get along with less knowledge by far than we seem prepared to give it credit for. Because it is an emblem of death, being both a jar of ashes and the "pictured urn" that pours out its imagery in Gray's "Progress," and thus empties its significance into life, the urn is the most ignorant of places, inferior in ignorance only to the "green altar" of human habitation because it is not made of leaves. Thus Keats answers the question of how poetry originates that is of such crucial concern in the ode tradition, clearly repeating what Wordsworth disclosed against his will in the Intimations ode: Death is the origin. Death begets the significance of which in itself, like an unmated family, it is quite barren.

# The "Ode on Indolence"

## Helen Vendler

The "Ode on Indolence," which Keats left unpublished, is, as Blackstone says, the seminal poem for the other great odes. Though it was written down as late as May, perhaps just before the "Ode on a Grecian Urn," since they share the same stanza (used afterward for the "Ode on Melancholy"), the experience which gave rise to it is related in March, in the March 19 section of Keats's journal-letter of February 14–May 3, 1819. The letter contains the imagery of the ode in little:

> This morning I am in a sort of temper indolent and supremely careless: I long after a stanza or two of Thompson's Castle of indolence . . . Neither Poetry, nor Ambition, nor Love have any alertness of countenance as they pass by me: they seem rather like three figures on a greek vase—a Man and two women— whom no one but myself could distinguish in their disguisement.

Keats later in the spring so reimagines himself into his March experience that he relives it among "the sweet tears of May"; nevertheless, the core of the ode remains his lassitude in March, his unwillingness to be roused out of his mysterious indolence by the three motives—Love, Ambition, and Poetry—which pass before him in Greek disguise.

The uneasy structure of "Indolence" enabled Charles Brown, copying probably from loose sheets, to propose an incorrect sequence for its stanzas, which he subsequently corrected; but only a poem peculiarly static could

From *The Odes of John Keats.* © 1983 by the President and Fellows of Harvard College. The Belknap Press of Harvard University Press, 1983.

have offered the possibility of such a mistake. In fact, the poem seems to make no apparent progress at all; as it begins, Keats is indolent; as it ends, he is indolent; the visit of the disturbing figures seems to have left him unchanged, an embryonic poet refusing to be born, nestled in the womb of preconscious existence.

The "Ode on Indolence," however, offers two conflicting structural shapes to our inspection: the first, attributable to the speaker, might properly be called by the Yeatsian name of vacillation; the second, a stronger shape of steady recurrence, attributable to the figures, counters the first. Though the ode does record a vacillation of Keatsian mood, ranging from languor to yearning, from self-reproach to self-indulgence (reinforced, as we shall see later, by its language), the stronger shape in the poem is the shape of recurrent return, as the three sculptural allegorical figures again and again intrude upon the varying Keatsian dream. In some ways the poem never recovers—never wishes to recover—from its sight of that spacious and unhurried Greek procession which entirely subdues the poet to its plastic grace:

> One morn before me were three figures seen,
>   With bowed necks, and joined hands, side-faced;
> And one behind the other stepp'd serene,
>   In placid sandals, and in white robes graced:
> They pass'd, like figures on a marble urn,
>   When shifted round to see the other side;
>     They came again; as when the urn once more
> Is shifted round, the first seen shades return;
>   And they were strange to me, as may betide
>     With vases, to one deep in Phidian lore.

Everything in the opening stanza reinforces the persistence and power of these art-figures, who so resemble the three Graces. They come not alone but companioned; their hands are joined in a unity of self-presentation; their movements are done in unison; they are dressed identically; at first sight they even seem identical as to sex. The theme of return is insisted on: "One behind the other *stepped* . . . / They *passed* . . . / They *came again*; as when . . . *once more* / . . . the *first* seen shades *return*." The poem continues to repeat this magic hovering of appearance and return in several rhetorical ways—by addressing the figures; by repeating their returns; by enumerating them (once in presence, once in absence) as Love, Ambition, and Poesy; by twice bidding them farewell; by entreating them to fade; by adjuring them to vanish. The whole poem is constructed upon their steady reappearances; as I have said, they make it, structurally speaking, a poem of recurrence.

Though Keats's attitude toward these presences changes with his changing epithets for them (they are to him first "figures," then "shadows," next "ghosts," and finally "phantoms"), they remain the same steady Greek forms, becoming, as they finally reveal their countenances to Keats, creations like Wallace Stevens's hidalgo on the stair, "a hatching that stared and demanded an answering look." Though begged by the poet to return to their places on the urn, though commanded to vanish into the clouds, they show no inclination to disappear or to discontinue their haunting of the indolent visionary.

Keats here deliberately presents himself, as he does in "Psyche," "Nightingale," and "Urn," as a poet. In this ode he speaks of his demon Poesy; in the others he refers to his "tuneless numbers," his "mused rhyme," and more generally in the "Urn" to "our rhyme." In "Indolence" the conflict between the claims of Poesy (accompanied by its motive, Ambition, and its subject, Love) and Keats's almost physical need for "indolence" seems insoluble. The figures, in their determination, are unpreventable and ungovernable, and cause recurrent agitation by each of their comings; and yet the claims of "indolence" are indisputable, and stubbornly reassert themselves against every reappearance of the Greek figures.

It is with the wisdom of hindsight—because we have read "Nightingale" and "Urn"—that we can see this conflict between form and indolence as if it were a battle between the two later odes. "Indolence" speaks with the tranced voice of the "Ode to a Nightingale"; the Greek figures, in their mute glance, evoke the language of the "Urn"; the one is the voice of the bower, the other the voice of the artifact. There is, of course, a third voice in "Indolence"—the voice which, awakened out of the bower and repudiating Greek gravity, speaks in the worldly-wise tones we associate with portions of *Lamia*:

> O folly! What is Love? and where is it?
> And for that poor Ambition—it springs
> From a man's little heart's short fever-fit.

We hear this affectedly cynical voice once more in "Nightingale": "The fancy cannot cheat so well / As she is fam'd to do, deceiving elf." Keats rejected these defensive tones as unworthy in the later odes, "Urn" and "Autumn"; there, bitterness and regret, the emotions underlying those cynical expressions, are allowed their proper undeflected voice, in the remarks on human passion and its aftermath in the one, and in the nostalgia for the songs of spring in the other.

In "Indolence," then, Keats tries the superposition of one structural shape on another; over the vacillating shape of the various resistances and yieldings of indolence to form, he places the steady recurrent shape of the rhythmic return of the Greek figures. Harold Bloom says very well that the three figures resembling the Graces are in fact Keats's Fates; we may therefore name the two rhythms as the rhythm of Fate superimposed on that of will. Each persists throughout the poem; but, as I have said, the inexplicable, prior, and beautiful appearance, at the opening of the poem, of the rhythm of Fate—for all the rebelliousness subsequently mustered against it—makes that rhythm in reality the eventual victor, or rather a victor whose eventual victory we find ourselves envisaging as the poem ends.

And yet—also with the wisdom of hindsight—we know that Keats had reason to prolong his state full of "visions for the night, / And for the day faint visions" (he changed the latter phrase to "waking dream" in "Nightingale"). It was during these waking trances and embowered sleeps that his powerful assimilations and creations first took on body and form. His hour of rendezvous with the urn has not yet come, he senses, and he wards it off, profitably, from March to May. The gestating indolence he insists on refuses any subjection to time; he is suspended in dream, as the sweet tears of May (later to fall in a weeping shower in "Melancholy") remain suspended in cloud in the sky. The season does not advance; he does not stir. The silent but urgent imperatives for change—Ambition, Love, and Poesy—challenge his immobility: his defensive impulse will be, in subsequent poems, to immobilize them in return, placing immobile Love in the center of his "Ode to Psyche," and immobile Love and Poesy at the center of the "Urn."

In this ode, then, we see the unwilling fancy of the artist facing at once its mental and emotional stimuli and its eventual sculptural artifact. The sculptural figures long to take on life, but are banished—back to the dreamy urn or up to the clouds, it scarcely matters—for the time being. The three spirits, almost indistinguishable each from the other, represent the principal dramatis personae of *Endymion* replicated in outline: the ambitious youth flanked by two maidens, one Love, the other Poesy, must recall to us Endymion placed between the Indian Maid and Cynthia. (Keats's letter had referred to the figures as "a Man and two women": in the ode Love and Poesy are clearly female, while Ambition is presumable male.) In short, the Fates here are Keats's doubling of his own dilemma of vocation already debated in *Endymion*, and the poem represents a dialogue of the embryonic, unformed, languorous, dreaming poetic self with its later envisaged incarnation in accomplished form.

Keats will never again incarnate form, or figures to be venerated, as an allegorical trinity. Ambition occurs, but incorporated into the speaker's own natural self, in *The Fall of Hyperion*; Love and Poesy are coupled as Cupid and Psyche in the "Ode to Psyche," which follows in inspiration the "Ode on Indolence." The two sculptural figures in "Psyche" are no longer allegorical representations of the poet's faculties for love and poesy, but rather have taken on separate mythological existence, an existence which for Cupid lapses somewhat at the end (where the poet seems to prepare to substitute himself for the god) but which is allowed throughout to Psyche. As a pagan goddess, Psyche preexisted, in the realm of mythology, her poet, and does not depend on him for her essence, as do the Love, Ambition, and Poesy of "Indolence." Keats's wish for an object of worship external to himself dictates several of his other later objects, henceforth single ones, of veneration—a bird, an urn, a season. Such choices, which go beyond an interest solely in an allegorical psychology of creation or in a mythological reading of existence, point, as I hope to show later, to Keats's interest in artifact, audience, and medium.

But in the "Ode on Indolence," the speaker is the indolent, inward-turned Keats still in his pastoral chrysalis, projecting onto an urn-*Doppelgänger* his internalized ambition, love, and poesy. The urn-double is unaffected by the expostulations of the protesting speaker: its figures return ever the same, ever poised, rhythmic, imperturbable, pregnant with meaning, placid, serene. In the top of sovereignty, these figures envisage all circumstance and remain unchanged under Keats's flurry of salutation, query, repudiation, and satire; their single gesture, a reproachful one, is to turn their profiles full face and force his acknowledgment of their acquaintance. And yet, in spite of the placidity of their circling, the figures are in themselves not entirely placid; pale-cheeked Ambition betrays the fatigue of long vigils (a link forward to Autumn's patient watching), and the demon Poesy is "most unmeek." One might say that, like a poem, they manifest recurrence of rhythm while encompassing interior agitation. In this dialogue of Keats's mind with itself, suffering finds no vent in action.

The poem turns on the visual pun between "idle" and "indolence." In the severe judgment of the expectant figures, Keats may be said to have an "idle spright"; in his own defensive judgment, he is merely steeped in summer "indolence." He wonders, seeing himself as a lily of the field, whether the emphasis of the figures on a "task" is not merely the Philistine advice of "busy common-sense." Conversely, in an apprehensive twinge of self-reproach, he even suspects them of deliberately muffling themselves up so that they might abandon him to his self-indulgence; he imagines them stealing away with hushed steps so as—in their fancied plot—to leave his "idle" days without a task to occupy them.

The preliminary passings of the figures allow such speculation. When the spirits seem not to be noticing him, Keats is piqued; when they *do* notice him, he feels—after a moment of wild yearning after them—that they have torn him from his obscurely necessary reverie. As we notice now the underlying shape —what I have called the shape of vacillation underlying the shape of figure-recurrence —the first thing we realize is that the language of Keats's indolence takes two forms, as he rebukes the soliciting figures: we may call these forms of language, for convenience, the "Nightingale"-form and the "Psyche"-form. The first speaks in terms of swoon, a numbness, and an insensibility; it sounds like a conflation of the opening drowsy numbness of the Nightingale ode with its subsequent blind sinking toward death:

> Ripe was the drowsy hour;
> The blissful cloud of summer-indolence
> Benumb'd my eyes; my pulse grew less and less;
> Pain had no sting, and pleasure's wreath no flower.
> O, why did ye not melt, and leave my sense
> Unhaunted quite of all but—nothingness?

In this mood, Keats praises "drowsy noons, / And evenings steep'd in honied indolence."

If this first exploration of indolence borrows that language of death, the second, in "Psyche"-language, borrows that of birth. The sleep, no longer one of oblivion, is instead one of rich dreams, growing flowers, a chiaroscuro of light and shade, all that "information (primitive sense)," as Keats called it in his last letter, taking place in a landscape of incipient emotion, open casements, new-leaved vines, budding warmth, and a singing thrush. The language of the open casement and the budding warmth is the language of "Psyche," just as Keats's self-stationing, his head "cool-bedded in the flowery grass," resembles his stationing of Cupid and Psyche, "couched side by side / In deepest grass . . . / 'Mid hush'd, cool-rooted flowers." The happy casement in "Psyche," open to let the warm Love in, will eventually become in "Nightingale" the magic casements framing no human figures, and opening on things perilous and forlorn; but here, in "Indolence," casements are still inviting, opening to press a leafy vine—

the vine not yet, as it will be later, loaded and blessed with fruit, but rather full of pure potentiality. The first, benumbed, variety of indolence is principally sketched from thoughts of death, insensibility, and dissolution; but the second, creative, indolence draws its imagery from thoughts of birth, humidity, emergence, and illumination. The second indolence is briefly anticipated in the opening adjectives of the first—"ripe" was the drowsy hour, "blissful" was the cloud; but then numbness and blankness supervene, and it is only later that the budding creative indolence is explored.

There are, in short, two indolent Keatses and one ambitious one in this poem. The first indolent one wishes to obliterate sensation and the senses, removing at one gesture both the sting of pain (and even the sting of death, whence he draws the phrase "pain's sting," we might guess, given the ode's biblical epigraph) and the flower of pleasure. But the second indolent Keats is overbrimmed with inner and outer sensations of the most exquisite sort, mixing the apprehension of May's tears with the luxuriating in flowers, budding warmth, light and shade, and the poetry of birdsong. The third Keats—the ambitious lover and aspiring poet—disturbs the repose of both his indolent selves, distracting the one from oblivion and the other from sensation and reverie. Each "indolent" objection to the admonitory figures is fully and satisfyingly voiced; but we see that the linked figures, beautiful as they are, have not yet found for themselves a language equal to the "indolent" poetry of sheathed sensation that in a single breath ensconces delicious feeling and embroidered dreams:

> My sleep had been embroider'd with dim dreams;
> My soul had been a lawn besprinkled o'er
> With flowers, and stirring shades, and baffled beams:
> The morn was clouded, but no shower fell,
> Though in her lids hung the sweet tears of May;
> The open casement press'd a new-leaved vine,
> Let in the budding warmth and throstle's lay.

Keats speaks so easily here of the fertile soul, its dreamy sleep and its germinating ground, intimate with such completions and interminglings, that the separate, austere, discarnate urn-figures can scarcely seem an intimate part of that soul or of its contents.

The "moral" argument of the ode pretends to see poetic ambition as a temptation toward praise, love as a temptation to sentimentality: "I would not be dieted with praise, / A pet-lamb in a sentimental farce!" But the weakness of the satiric writing betrays Keats's inability to dismiss the true and justified sense of his own genius, and the intensity of his own passionate

...ent. What was preventing his acquiescence in the demands of the figures was—though he could scarcely have known it in March—the incompleteness of those early dreams (including this dream of a rather unimaginatively decorated urn) which would yield, in a few weeks, the great odes.

If we recapitulate Keats's state of feeling in March (assuming that the ode is a reconstruction of his mind at the time), we find that his most powerful feelings were those of rapturous sensations both mental and physical, which took the form of sensing things beginning and about to happen—flowers budding, shades stirring, sunbeams seeking a path, tears about to fall, opening windows, bare vines growing green, warmth, birdsong, the vague shapes of night visions and waking dreams in daytime. These feelings are combated by an unwillingness to feel such new stirrings, a wish to sink into insensibility (prompted, we might suppose, by the illness of Tom Keats and his death a few months earlier on December 1). Keats is also tempted to repudiate as worthless all his dearest desires—for fame, for love, for poetry; and yet he feels a steady and unyielding pursuit of his attention by his poetic genius, which will not be denied no matter how often he refuses its solicitations and banishes it (together with all stirrings of ambition and love) from his presence. He senses his poetic genius as another self, moving in mysterious and separate recurrences quite without reference to earthly time, displaying always a dignity and serenity of purpose, and emerging somehow from the noblest examples of creation he had seen, the Phidian marbles. He feels irrepressibly his own vocation as artificer, worker in a medium, one whose destined creations have come from their matrix (here, from an as yet unrealized "dreamy" urn) to rebuke their creator for not yet having created them. They bear, for that reason, overtones of the haunting ghost of old Hamlet rebuking his son for not yet having entered upon action.

In spite of the beauty of the rich language of open casements, cloud-tears, dreams, a bird's "lay," and vegetative growth—a garden of Adonis for the odes later conceived—the single most memorable moment in "Indolence" comes, surprisingly, in the poet's penitent "How is it, shadows, that I knew ye not?" The pang of that self-address (since the qualities Keats "knew not" were his own) is the kernel of feeling from which the whole ode originates, representing the pain of the accusatory encounter which is the subject of the ode, and the pain that the poet feels at his own ignorance in the encounter. He did not know his own soul, not when it appeared before him in that strange trio conjoining a processional rhythm with maiden fairness, fatigued eye, pallid cheek, and demonic fancy. Not to know one's own soul is for Keats the most mortal of lapses; he cannot believe that he has not recognized himself in this objectified vision. It becomes clear in the course of the ode that he has not known the shadows because he did not wish to know them, and this refusal had been prompted on the one hand by an exhausted shrinking from all further experience, painful and pleasurable alike, and on the other by an inchoate, if deeply felt, need for a longer time of budding and ripening. The hint of deathliness in the three figures, as they are evoked by the successively more disembodied names of shadows, ghosts, and phantoms, points to the degree to which sensual life must be sacrificed in being mediated into art-figuration; but Keats is not yet willing to explore his instinct for the inseparability of creation and sacrifice.

If we turn to look more closely at the language of the ode, we see that it uneasily adopts at least four modes of speech: narration of a past event to a presumed reader ("One morn before me were three figures seen"); recollection of the past event in a dreamy self-reverie ("Ripe was the drowsy hour"); an address (in the present tense) to the figures seen in the past ("How *is* it, shadows that I *knew* ye not?"); and agitated worldly inter-polation, occurring in the latter half of the poem only ("O folly! What is Love? and where is it?"). There is a marked unsettling of consciousness as Keats passes from one form of speech to the other. It may be most visible in the affected Byronic dismissal of Love and Ambition, but it is no less disturbing, if better managed, in the transitions from narration to recol-lection, from recollection to direct address, and so on. The poem exhibits Keats's problems in composition, problems occasioned by a wish to be fair, at one and the same time, to all sides of his nature and his art. Once he has decided on the visionary *donnèe* of the poem, he feels compelled to explain his ghostly procession to those not so privileged, thus generating the heavy-handed narration of the ode, so much more swiftly accomplished in its original allegorical and nonvisionary form in the journal-letter. In the letter he feels no obligation to claim any status as seer or sage; but to authenticate in the poem his vision and his original bafflement, he feels it necessary to establish his *bona fides* as an interpreter of Greek figures (he is learned, he tells his reader, in statues, but has not yet progressed beyond "Phidian" lore to an expertise with vase conventions). All this narration and expla-nation is incurred for the benefit of a putative listener to Keats's flowery tale, since Keats would not need to tell himself again how many times the figures passed, or why he did not recognize the iconography of vase dec-oration, or what his credentials in interpretation might be.

Quite another motive from the explanatory one lies behind the powerful and sensual recreation of the drowsy hour, the most successful "writing"—in the limited sense of "intense, magical, and profound use of language"—in the poem. It is my aim here to insist on a larger sense of "writing" in Keats—a sense which will include the grander issues of poetic conceptualization and architectonics as well as "magical" language—but every reader's first response to Keats (and many readers' final response) rests on judgments of his success or failure at the level of intensity or adequacy of language at any given instant, and on that alone. At any given instant, however, besides finding the *mot juste*, Keats is also deciding on a means of conceptualization (as, here, he has decided for three figures, which change conceptually from figures to phantoms, and from profiled figures to full-face figures); and at any given instant, he is also deciding how to continue, delay, or complete the structure of his poem (here, by the device of successive apparitions). The invention of appropriate language, in short, is only one of many inventions. Two others, invention of concept and invention of structure, are equally important in the odes, even if they have so far, by comparison to "writing" *tout court*, been comparatively neglected in criticism.

Since the most adequate language Keats finds in "Indolence" is the language for private re-creation of the scene of indolence (the language of private memory and reverie, not directed to an audience), I take it as axiomatic that the kernel of the poem, as a crystallization of accomplished feeling, lies in these passages. This does not prevent the competing kernel—a crystallization, in the figures, of a will for future accomplishment—from claiming entire emotional authenticity as well; but it is an authenticity for which a style has yet to be found. The restless stirrings of the will for accomplishment motivate all modes of speech here except the re-creative indolent one. But is it to that re-creative one, with its two facets of deathliness and ripening, that I wish now to turn.

The note of re-creation enters with the blended richness of two Keatsian themes—growth and sleep—in "Ripe was the drowsy hour," a line apparently promising both fruit and dream-visions. But we are balked of both as the first facet of indolence is momentarily turned to us—the apparent death of the senses, as they sink into an unconsciousness of almost all stimuli, "unhaunted quite of all but nothingness." It is, as we know, the vision of the three figures which prevents the poet's senses from that absolute annihilation. Keats's language for the negation of sense in sleep is fatally contaminated here with the luxuriousness of sense: it is far from the withered sedge and from places where no birds sing. Something very rich in his indolence is struggling for expression behind these negations. If his eyes are benumbed, it is by a *blissful* cloud; his pulse lessens by *growing* (even if by growing less and less); the two interpolated "no's" can scarcely obliterate the main nouns clustered in "pain . . . sting . . . pleasure's wreath . . . flower"; and the sweet and joyful steeping of evenings in honeyed indolence cannot be thought to represent a "nothingness."

In passing to the second, more openly creative facet of indolence, the activities of the "soul" when we are laid asleep in body, Keats borrows from "Tintern Abbey" a Wordsworthian division of body and soul which will not, in the long run, prove congenial to him. The philosophical Wordsworthian language for what happens when we are laid asleep in body and become a living soul is an impossible idiom for Keats; his soul, in its activities, is indistinguishable from his senses. The promise in "Ripe was the drowsy hour" now becomes fulfilled in dream, blossom, and song, in the most accomplished lines of the ode. In this fifth stanza, the "dim dreams" of the indolent soul borrow their language proleptically from the "dreamy urn"; the "stirring shades" within the soul's garden are named almost cunningly from "the first seen shades" of the urn-figures; the "besprinkled . . . flowers" arise from the repudiated "flower" of pleasure's wreath; the "clouded" morn in the awakened, if dreaming, soul is born from the "blissful cloud" of summer indolence numbing the eyes of sense; and, in the most evident parallel of all, the "tears of May" gather above those unshed "tears of mine," as the poet calls them, which he would refuse to have shed at the adieu of the figures (or so he boasts), had they consented to retreat, and leave him undisturbed.

The invasion, then, of the diction of the deep soul-dream by the diction of externality (whether of the external figures or the surrounding landscape) is proof that the soul-dream cannot remain sheltered from the world of time (the changing of the moons) and human "annoy" (pain and pleasure alike). "The voice of busy common-sense" (which we may call a denigration of the voice of mind in its pragmatic mood) Keats will not here dignify by conceptualizing it into a figure. But he does conceptualize the three other figures of "annoy"—Love, Ambition, and Poesy—and the problems of conceptualization provoke equal problems of diction.

In the journal-letter, the figures are psychological motives, externalized because at the moment they are being rejected, or defended against; and their allegorization comes in a simile of appeal and detachment at once; the motives are contemplated but they are inert, having no "alertness of countenance," and seeming "like three figures on a greek vase." The externality and lifelessness of the motives do not survive their poetic reification into visionary forms: though they begin in placidity and serenity, they quickly arrive at disquieting, if disguised, intent; and one, the "demon Poesy," takes on an "unmeek" power rather like that of Lamia, who seemed "some demon's mistress, or the demon's self" (*Lamia*, 1, 56). The changing vocatives to the figures, and the uncertainty of conceptualization, suggest that Keats was not entirely master of the evolution of the poem.

Keats's suspicion of the figures yields the first tentative conceptualization of their function. Have they muffled themselves to steal away from him unrecognized, and leave him unmanned, without a task? Are they plotters against him, disguising their deep and silent plotting? Beholding one's own former energizing motives while refusing to acknowledge their present claim is the experience described in the journal-letter: Keats's change of nonacknowledgment to nonrecognition compels an ascription of intent to the reified motives which is not, in terms of the fiction of the poem, entirely coherent, since Keats seems both to desire and to repudiate a task in one breath. As I have said earlier, it is the conflict of "idleness" (as both the voice of busy common sense and the voice of the figures, if they had one, would seem to call it) and "indolence" (as the voice of creative patience would call it) which is in question; but the melodramatic and theatrical diction of muffled shadows engaged in a deep-disguised plot, while it may be summoned up by those memories of Shakespeare, particularly *Hamlet*, which lie behind several of the odes, is a diction wholly unsuitable as a mode of address to urn-figures, and it vanishes leaving not a trace behind.

The reproachful "haunting" which seems the main intent of the figures links them, for Keats, with the ghost of Hamlet's father, with his purposeful remanifesting of himself to his indolent son; the figures are therefore invoked in purgatorial epithets suitable to revenants or shades. On the other hand, they are also life-figures, secular motives from the world of pain and pleasure, and to describe them Keats borrows, in an explanatory fashion connected with his narration to a common reader, diction from the common stock of emblematic moral iconography, to which he will again resort in the "Ode to a Nightingale." Love the "fair maid" and Ambition "pale of cheek, / And ever watchful with fatigued eye" belong to the same static frieze of commonplaces on which we can see palsy shaking "a few, sad, last gray hairs," and men sitting and hearing each other groan. These fixed emblems evoke in every case Keats's feeblest diction precisely because they are representative of fixed and received ideas. He cannot bring himself to resort to one of these emblems for Poesy, at least not here in the ode. In the letter, Poetry had been as inert as Ambition or Love; but here Poesy takes on incremental life; the more blame is heaped on her, the more Keats loves her, a process mimicked by the phrase "more, the more . . . , most" incorporated into the stanza.

Keats first conceptualized the figures as graceful unknown visitors, next as theatrical muffled plotters, next as reproachful revenants, and next as moral emblems of duty or desire; his last conceptualization of them, and in the event his governing one, is as deities. The figures become the gods who preside over the ode, refusing to be dismissed by the speaker, for all his adjurations to them to fade and vanish. Protests are in vain; Keats might say of them, as Yeats does of his Magi:

> Now as at all times I can see in the mind's eye,
> In their stiff, painted clothes, the pale unsatisfied ones
> Appear and disappear.

One of Keats's difficulties with the conceptualization of his unsatisfied ones is that they represent such different internalized objects of the self. Love represents the erotic object, Ambition the social object, and Poesy the creative object: these figures are at once self-projections (Keats as a lover, as fame-seeker, and as poet) and internalized objects. Ambition belongs at least in part to the world of busy common sense and sentimental farce; Love, Keats fears, belongs especially to the world where change the moons; and Poesy, he suspects, belongs to a world more demonic than pastoral. But besides being self-projections (Love and Poesy, by convention "unmanly," must be projected as female beloved and female Muse) and internalized objects, these figures are, in the Keatsian sense, "presiders," as Shakespeare was to Keats a presider. Their elevated state dictates Keats's elevated language of address, different from the conversational narration ("One morn before me") or the affectedly colloquial language of expostulation ("and, forsooth! I wanted wings") or the dreamy language of sensual luxury in spiritual germination (evoked by the "lawn besprinkled o'er / With flowers"). The elevated diction does not preclude intimacy ("How is it, shadows, that I knew ye not?"), accusation ("O, why did ye not melt?"), or defiance ("Ye cannot raise / My head cool-bedded in the flowery grass"). But each time Keats moves into direct address to the deities (away from description, recollection, or social expostulation), the temperature of the poem rises in what we may call odal fire, a very different temperature from the incubating vernal warmth of the re-creative stanzas. By reducing the number of persons addressed and by keeping direct address throughout, Keats made the later odes more coherent than "Indolence," with its three addressees only intermittently addressed.

In its passages from first-person narration to second-person address and back again, "Indolence" is unique among the odes, as "Melancholy" is unique in never addressing its presiding deity, but rather being a second-person address to the poet's own self. In the other odes, the deity—whether soul-goddess ("Psyche"), artist ("Nightingale"), art-object ("Urn"), or season ("Autumn")—is unfailingly the object of address. In fact, Keats's largest single aesthetic decision in writing the greater odes was to place them squarely in the poetic tradition of invocation and prayer, where he had placed the first of his ambitious odes, the hymn to Pan in the first book of *Endymion*. (The later ode sung by the Indian Maid to Sorrow, in book 4, mixes narration and invocation, and includes, in its incorporated vision of a Bacchic procession, interrogations of attendant damsels and satyrs prefiguring the interrogation of the figures on the urn.) The second firm aesthetic decision Keats made in the later odes was to speak in *propria persona*—not through a dramatic character like the Indian Maid, not in the choral unison of worshipers as in the hymn to Pan, but in his own troubled and aspiring single voice. Even when he mentions "other woe than ours" or "breathing human passion," the voice that utters those words is not the voice of a chorus or of humanity in general but that of a single speaker. Keats's third great decision, having adopted his single speaker, was to minimize the role of that speaker in successive odes until, from the visible single poet in "Indolence," "Psyche," and "Nightingale," he has become the self-effacing and anonymous speaker, not specified as a poet, of "Autumn."

The Byronic language of irony, which, as I have said, appears briefly in "Indolence," is motivated no less by Keats's defensive guilt at the approach of the figures than by his own leap of the heart as he wishes to follow them: "I burn'd / And ached for wings." The motive of self-distrust rarely yields good poetry in Keats, and will fade from the odes, but this instance of it heralds the later outburst against the cheating Fancy, the cold Pastoral, and the inaccessible Melancholy (in the canceled first stanza of that ode). All of these testify to the hostile energies released (after an attempt at idealization, invocation, or transcendence) by the journey homeward to habitual self. Until the motive of these necessary journeys homeward can be incorporated into the motive of idealization itself (and this does not happen until the close of "Melancholy"), the intemperate diction of disillusion must, if Keats is to remain truthful to his own emotions, confront the ecstatic or worshipful or in any case invocational diction provoked by the divine or idealized object.

We can see, in the concluding stanza of "Indolence," all of Keats's previously established modes of speech jostling each other in an uncomfortable medley—the invocational ("So, ye three ghosts, adieu!"), the indolent re-creative ("my head cool-bedded in the flowery grass"), the ironic and hostile ("A pet-lamb in a sentimental farce!"), the descriptive-narrative ("masque-like figures on the dreamy urn"), the deprecatory language critical of sensation ("my idle spright"), and the language for the as yet discarnate stirrings of the will ("I yet have visions"). Eventually his boast that "for the day faint visions there is store" will be abundantly manifest in "Autumn," her "store" anything but faint; but for the moment the claim is asserted only, its fruit invisible.

I cannot forbear to add a note on sentence rhythm, because Keats is quickened into different syntactic rhythms by his different languages. The stately pentameter passage of the first quatrain of the ode is somewhat dulled in the rather pedestrian repetitions of the following four lines; a new note of beauty is not discovered until the re-creative series of clauses is ushered in with the medial trochaic inversion "Ripe was the drowsy hour," and a waywardness of phrasal rhythm (which I reproduce here) begins to please the ear:

> Ripe was the drowsy hour;
> The blissful cloud of summer-indolence benumb'd my eyes;
> My pulse grew less and less;
> Pain had no sting, and pleasure's wreath no flower.

Though this is not an exquisite progression, the last line being too sententiously phrased for the state of soul it wishes to express, there is a kinetic deployment of rhythm which turns the pentameter away from stateliness and into a pulse of breathing irregularity. A religious formality resumes with "A third time pass'd they by," and then rhythmic inventiveness flags in the entirely too programmatic enumeration of the allegorical figures, with one line given to Love, two to Ambition, and predictably three to Poesy, a pattern repeated in the subsequent repudiation of the figures, which again reserves one line for the refusal of Love, two for Ambition, and three for Poesy. Rhythmic inventiveness recurs only in the second scene of re-creation, after which Keats resorts to a rhythm more or less confined to simple pentameter, in which syntax is accommodated to metrical form.

The diction of re-creation, in which Keats, after his exercises in *Endymion*, is already wholly accomplished, is a sensual diction (even if it is used, as it is here, to describe a spiritual state in which the senses themselves are benumbed and the pulse is lessened). Its elements include, as in so many other passages we shall encounter, drowsiness, ripeness, honey, dreams, a chiaroscuro (here of "stirring shades, and baffled beams"), flowers, grass, moisture, clouds, a personified time (which can be a month or season, here May with her "sweet tears" and morn with her "lids" in which raindrops hang as tears), an open casement, leaves, buds, warmth, and bird-song. This moist, sensual complex exists in conjunction (sometimes in competition) with a complex associated with idealization; some of its elements include stone (here an urn; elsewhere an altar or steps), figuration (here the urn-shades), dance, masque, or procession (here the joined hands and the serene pace), wings (as here, Keats would need wings to follow the figures), and architectural enclosure. Clouds, as the source of natural moisture and the realm of divine habitation, are common to both clusters of imagery; and dreams or visions seem, though springing from the one realm of indolence, to engender the other, that of idealization. All of these images will recur, and be amplified, and reduced, and reaffirmed, and criticized, in the later odes.

Keats searches in "Indolence" for a proper mode of self-cognition. The speaking "I" wishes, for the moment, to know itself solely as a being in gestation, one whose senses have been laid to sleep and whose soul is an indolent lawn full of restless glimmers, dreamy budding, warmth, and overheard song. It does not wish to know itself in its erotic role as lover, its social role as seeker for fame, or its creative role as poet. It arduously repudiates the possibility that it may incarnate itself in an artifact. These questions of self-definition—in roles passive, active, erotic, social, and creative—will persist through the odes. "Indolence" is too timid even to take credit for its own visions: the figures come not by being summoned but rather appear inconclusively veiled in the passive: "One morn before me *were* three figures *seen* . . . / They pass'd like figures on a marble urn, / When *shifted* round . . . / They came again; as when the urn once more / Is *shifted* round." "Indolence" 's dual projection of the Keatsian self—into drowsy vegetative nature and into stern Greek figures—will also recur in the odes, as tension, as problem, and ultimately as solution.

We are left, in the end, with the two rhythms of the poem. One of them, the recurrent processional stateliness (as, in the manner of a charm, three figure come three times), is the rhythm of an embodied art and a compelling Fate. It is counterpointed, no less intensely, by the other, fitful, rhythm of refusal—now refusing in a lethargic lessened pulse, now in a rather uneasy cynicism, now in a ripeness of sensation and faint vision. In spite of his putative indolence, the poet is forcefully drawn into a relation with the allegorical figures, abruptly and briefly in the first, disturbed, address, posing the profound question of self-cognition—"How is it, shadows, that I knew ye not?"—and, again in a more prolonged way, in the repeated farewells which close the poem:

> O shadows! 'twas a time to bid farewell!
>
> . . . . . . . . . . . . . . . .
>
> So, ye three ghosts, adieu!
>
> . . . . . . . . . .
>
> Fade softly from my eyes
>
> . . . . . . . . . . .
>
> Farewell! I yet have visions
>
> . . . . . . . . . . .
>
> Vanish, ye phantoms

These farewells and adieux place the poet in the position of an impotent magus or a would-be Prospero summoning and dismissing spirits. We see that these spirits will not be dismissed, that Keats has raised himself, in his dispute with them, from indolence. He begins to command his spiritual world even in attempting to refuse it; though he has not yet conceptualized its demands (which he will later call Beauty and Truth), he has conceptualized its aims (to love, to be ambitious for greatness, to be a poet). He remains, for the moment, the artist shrinking from embodying his faint vegetative visions in anything resembling an artifact, refusing even the purely mental cultivation of Fancy (in which he will take such active pleasure in "Psyche"). In making the constitutive rhetorical figure of "Indolence" that of dialectic, or dispute, Keats proposes an art of inconclusiveness: the rhetorical shape of the poem is that of a stalemate—nothing, neither way. The budding warmth of spiritual sensuality refuses to the end the cold pastoral of art; but the very insistence of the pressure toward figuration makes the shape of dispute seem a disingenuous one. The language, too, offers an unresolved conflict between the deathly and the lifelike; one scarcely knows whether the figures are more or less alive than the throstle. What is clear is that the budding natural warmth of this ode does not at all yet see its way clear to becoming an aesthetic warmth, in "the way some pictures look warm," which will so mercifully enable the composition of "To Autumn." Keats, like his later bees, hopes in this poem that warm days will never cease; but the figures—silent, gentle, but persistent—have come to tell him otherwise.

# Silent Forms: The "Ode to Psyche" and the "Ode on a Grecian Urn"

## Martin Aske

In this [essay] I should like to concentrate primarily on the "Ode to Psyche" and the "Ode on a Grecian Urn," with briefer detours through the projected but unfinished ode, "Mother of Hermes! and still youthful Maia!," and the "Ode on Indolence." Composed shortly after the abandonment of *Hyperion* in the spring of 1819, the "Ode to Psyche" and the "Ode on a Grecian Urn" continue to situate, in a different form, the problem of antiquity's representation, which had shaped both *Hyperion* and *Endymion*. Keats now returns to the dominant trope of the early sonnets of Chapman's Homer and the Elgin Marbles, the drama of an encounter between the poet and the forms of antiquity, with its attendant shock and suggestion of epiphany. There is, however, no simple return from narrative to lyric; Keats endeavours "to circumvent the sonnet (now so habitual to him) and to develop a longer, more flexible form." We might go further and propose that, in the longer and more flexible form of the "Ode on a Grecian Urn," in particular, the poet supplements *Hyperion* by turning to explore the very conditions of narrative. Interrupting Keats's brief epic, the ode might be read as a prologue to what might be possible for a narrative representation of antiquity. It traces the difficult emergence of rhetoric itself, in relation to the fictions and images which it desires to reinscribe in a modern text.

Or the odes might be viewed as standing to *Hyperion* in the same way that Milton's sonnets, according to Hazlitt, stand to *Paradise Lost*: "They are like tender flowers that adorn the base of some proud column or stately temple." As floral embellishments to the broken monument of *Hyperion*,

From *Keats and Hellenism: An Essay*. © 1985 by Cambridge University Press.

the odes shape a parergonal metacommentary on the failure of narrative to reanimate the ancient fictions.

Psyche, latest and loveliest of the Olympians, is a parergonal figure, insofar as her relation to the "work" (the poem) is always tangential, never wholly accomplished. Like the Grecian urn, she is a figuration of antiquity, an emblem of Keats's supreme fiction. Yet Lemprière reminds us that "Psyche is generally represented with the wings of a butterfly," and in the ode Psyche will indeed be as elusive as the butterfly in *Endymion*, ever likely to disappear "fairy-quick" (2, 93). The poet's representation of Psyche is further complicated by the fact that she is a belated member of the classical Pantheon: "You must recollect that Psyche was not embodied as a goddess before the time of Apuleius the Platonist who lived after the Augustan age, and consequently the Goddess was never worshipped or sacrificed to with any of the ancient fervour—and perhaps never thought of in the old religion." This might explain why the poet turns to Psyche as his mediator with antiquity: "As a human 'goddess' too late for the glory of mythology, Psyche is a perfect figure for Keats's own belated age." Psyche, then, would seem to be a particularly appropriate emblem through which the poet might define his relation to antiquity. But Psyche eludes representation. Keats speaks of her "embodied as a goddess," yet the "Ode to Psyche" fails to embody its shaping fiction, just as the "Ode on a Grecian Urn" will fail to embody the urn and its "leaf-fring'd legend." Despite the eagerness of the poet's "greeting of the Spirit," which is required for "things semireal . . . to make them wholly exist," Psyche will emerge into the poem tenuously and, in the end, ironically. In a typically fertile sentence, Hazlitt observed of Raphael's depiction of Cupid and Psyche (on the ceiling of the Farnesina Palace in Rome) that the artist "surpassed himself in a certain swelling and voluptuous grace, as if beauty grew and ripened under his touch, and the very genius of ancient fable hovered over his enamoured pencil." Raphael, evidently, was able to confer sensuous form on the hovering genius of ancient fable. But Keats's poem, equally enamoured of the ancient fictions, is scarcely able to contain Psyche in the same way; her presence seems indeed to hover in the text without ever settling and establishing itself. Thus we find the "winged Psyche" in a hovering embrace with Cupid: "Their lips touch'd not, but had not bade adieu" (17). "Fluttering among the faint Olympians" (42), Psyche hovers between presence and absence, inside and outside, on the borders of the poet's mind and of the text itself. To invoke her as the "brightest" of the Olympians is, within the poem's complex irony, a rhetorical strategy designed to conceal the shadowy vagueness of Psyche, her opacity and elusiveness. Or else her brightness, like the brightness of Cynthia and Lamia, threatens overexposure of the image, its withdrawal into blank invisibility.

The Grecian urn, on the other hand, appears to be Keats's most concrete and determinate emblem of antiquity. Do we not think of it as a specific image, a tangible object, a rounded whole with shape and substance? This, at least, is evident from the kind of criticism which has desired to place Keats's poem in the tradition of *ekphrasis*, "the poetic description of a pictorial or sculptural work of art." But the poem, I would say, is anything but a simple "description," or "verbal transposition of the sensuous appearance of a Greek urn." For the urn will tease both poet and reader to the extent that it refuses to be aligned with any such tradition. To describe and transpose is precisely what the poem's discourse fails to do; it can only question and hesitatingly surmise. Burdened by the familiar difficulty of representation, discourse can scarcely release the urn into the riper dimensions of sensuous, objective being. "Most of the odes," says Geoffrey Hartman, "are a feverish quest to enter the life of a pictured scene, to be totally where the imagination is." This would seem particularly true of the "Ode on a Grecian Urn." For Keats, however, the scene of antiquity always threatens to turn into a screen, a blankness that obscures the poet's sight (site) of his supreme fiction. Far from providing "the classic example of iconic verse," the ode remains fraught with difficulty in its "picture-pondering," as the poet seeks vainly to enter the landscape of his imaginary scene.

## II

The opening lines of the "Ode to Psyche" imagine an exclusive intimacy between poet and goddess:

> O Goddess! hear these tuneless numbers, wrung
>     By sweet enforcement and remembrance dear,
> And pardon that thy secrets should be sung
>     Even into thine own soft-conched ear.
>
> (1–4)

And the subsequent tableau, of Psyche and Cupid "couched side by side / In deepest grass"(9–10), might be read as an elaborate fantasy of this desired intimacy between poet and muse (in his commentary on Apuleius's version of the fable of Cupid and Psyche, Thomas Taylor observed that Psyche's "invisible husband" is a symbol of "pure *desire*"). But we find the poet's "tuneless numbers" curiously echoing back the goddess's "secrets," as though these secrets which the goddess had presumably passed on to the privileged poet could only ever be relayed back to the goddess's "soft-conched ear." If Psyche is the source of quasi-divine secrets, the fits of inspiration which she bestows on the poet seems only able to express itself as repetition—not repetition in a finer tone, but a repetition which is "tuneless," less fine than the original. The rest of the poem seeks to liberate itself from the potential sterility of tuneless repetition, yet it will only be able to do so by elevating the poet's own voice at the expense of Psyche's.

The "Ode to Psyche" and the "Ode on a Grecian Urn" both disclose the poet's desire to make his supreme fiction audible; in each case, however, it is the poet's own voice which must somehow compensate for the object's intractable silence. The ode *manqué*, "Mother of Hermes! and still youthful Maia!," also reflects a concern for voice, and it may at this point be useful to see how this fragment resolves the poet's appeal to antiquity.

Again the text yields a hint of the poet's desire for intimacy with the object of his apostrophe:

> Mother of Hermes! and still youthful Maia!
>    May I sing to thee
> As thou wast hymned on the shores of Baiae?
>    Or may I woo thee
> In earlier Sicilian? or thy smiles
> Seek, as they once were sought, in Grecian isles,
> By bards who died content in pleasant sward,
>    Leaving great verse unto a little clan?
>
>                      (1–8)

The poet pretends that for his serenade there are options from which he might choose: should he adopt the voice of Virgil, or Theocritus, or Homer? It seems to be a question of finding a voice to which Maia will respond most readily, for she is, after all, an object which must be wooed and sought. In which case Maia is, despite the presumption of intimacy, no more a given presence in the poem than Psyche is in the "Ode to Psyche." Rather she might be an object of desire who needs to be coaxed into presence through the poet's own voice. Yet even in this brief fragment the desire itself takes on a complex form. The poem's first line harks back, obliquely, to the final moment of "I stood tip-toe upon a little hill," "Was there a Poet born?"(241). If Maia is the mother of Hermes, and yet "still youthful," might she not also be the mother of the poet himself, and allow him to be reborn into the Arcadian realm of those bards "who died content in pleasant sward"? In his imagination the poet becomes another Hermes, who was born, Lemprière tells us, in Arcadia, and to whom "the invention of the lyre and its seven strings is ascribed." At the same time, however, the poem's language generates from within itself a different movement. The echo of "Maia" in the repeated "May I," as well as the insistent sound of "I" in the rhymes "Maia" / "Baiae," "smiles" / "isles," "By . . . died," help to readjust the relation of goddess and poet, not in terms of mother and child, but indeed as the very opposite. On the level of sound "Maia" herself is actually reborn out of the repetition of "May I"—*that* is how her presence is established, in the rhetorical act of the poet's song.

In this sense, Maia and Psyche both stand in the same ambivalent relation to the poet. As classical fictions they are objects of desire which always seem to hover beyond the reach of the modern poet. As a way, therefore, of coming to terms with their irreducible elusiveness, the poet elaborates a compensatory fiction—the fiction that goddess or muse is finally dependent for her very existence on the authority of the poet's voice.

But this fiction works more successfully (and more ironically) in the "Ode to Psyche" than in the "Mother of Hermes!" fragment. The "Ode to Psyche" is a true ode insofar as it becomes a celebration; it celebrates the authority of the poet's own voice. But it is precisely here where the shorter text ceases to be an ode, and turns into an elegy. Whereas the poet's voice in the "Ode to Psyche" gradually gains dominance, the poet's song in "Mother of Hermes!" is finally imagined as dying away. "O give me their old vigour"(9), pleads the poet; but rather than "great verse" the bards' "old vigour" inspires a song that is scarcely heard, an echo already on the point of dying away ("die away," at the end of line 12, itself dies away in the poem's concluding cadence, "a day"). "Content as theirs, / Rich in the simple worship of a day"(13–14): although these concluding lines seem to register a tranquil assurance that the poet's song could indeed have participated in some kind of plenitude generated by "old vigour," this is felt at the very moment of the song's—and the poem's—extinction. The delicate conjunction of the ideas of death and "Rich" anticipates a more famous moment in the "Ode to a Nightingale": "Now more than ever seems it rich to die"(55). In both cases the moment is "rich" because it bears witness to a plenitude on the verge of dissolving into the vacancy of death.

One might say, then, that the poem's formal incompleteness endorses its theme—"Mother of Hermes!" remains a fragment precisely because the poet's song has died away. Whereas the fragment of *Hyperion* pauses on the threshold of the poet's imaginative (re)birth (Apollo's dying into life), this fragment collapses the poet's birth and the death of his song into one brief moment. Any sense of prolonged imaginative life nourished by the classical fictions is elided in the poem's fragmentary form.

As I have suggested, the poet's voice in the "Ode to Psyche" does not die away, but rather increases in volume and authority. For all the conventional homage paid to her as a goddess, Psyche may be nothing more than an eloquent projection of the poet's voice, or, to put it another way, "a pure creation of the poet's brain." Psyche will be redeemed, but redeemed through rhetoric alone.

The second stanza is notable for its obvious and less obvious repetitions:

> O latest born and loveliest vision far
>   Of all Olympus' faded hierarchy!
> Fairer than Phoebe's sapphire-region'd star,
>   Or Vesper, amorous glow-worm of the sky;
>   Fairer than these.
>
> (24–28)

In the eyes of the poet, Psyche is, apparently, the fairest of them all. Yet an element of doubt about this statement creeps in when we remind ourselves that the repetition of "Fairer" comes close to flattery (or consolation), and that we still hear in "Fairer" the immediately preceding sounds of "faded" and "far," hinting that Psyche is still sufficiently distant to require a strenuous rhetorical effort on the part of the poet to bring her closer. Psyche's absence is then signified through a series of metonymic substitutions:

> though temple thou has none,
>   Nor altar heap'd with flowers;
> Nor virgin-choir to make delicious moan
>   Upon the midnight hours;
> No voice, no lute, no pipe, no incense sweet
>   From chain-swung censer teeming;
> No shrine, no grove, no oracle, no heat
>   Of pale-mouth'd prophet dreaming.
>
> (28–35)

Psyche's absence is conveyed through the repetition of negatives, "none," "Nor," "no," and through the overdetermination of the apostrophic "O" which ushers in this stanza and the next one as well ("O," the echo of "no," is the cipher of absence, as it will also be in the "Ode on a Grecian Urn"). But it is in the next stanza that the movement of negation and absence is halted and reversed by the intervention of "I," the mark of the

poet's voice. The presence of "I" is already implied in the repeated asso-
nances of "brightest," "lyre," "fire," "retir'd," before finally coming to
the surface here: "I sing, and sing, by my own eyes inspired"(43). The
extraordinary internal repetition of "I" in this line serves to establish the
poet's authority once and for all. At the beginning of the ode the poet had
been seen in a conventional posture of humility towards his muse; now he
is fully in command. Even the subsequent repetition of "Thy" in the rest
of the stanza has the ironic rhetorical effect of echoing insistently the presence of "I."

So it seems that the only way to brighten the faint Olympians is for
the poet to assert his own visionary and vocal authority. Yet this declaration
of power has ambivalent consequences. The poet claims to be Psyche's
champion, yet his benevolence is that of the despot. Psyche remains silently
subservient, while the poet usurps the privilege of discourse; he is compelled to speak for his object, in the only way that remains available to his
belated condition:

> Yes, I will be thy priest, and build a fane
> In some untrodden region of my mind,
> Where branched thoughts, new grown with pleasant pain,
> Instead of pines shall murmur in the wind:
> Far, far around shall those dark-cluster'd trees
> Fledge the wild-ridged mountains steep by steep;
> And there by zephyrs, streams, and birds, and bees,
> The moss-lain Dryads shall be lull'd to sleep;
> And in the midst of this wide quietness,
> A rosy sanctuary will I dress
> With the wreath'd trellis of a working brain,
> With buds, and bells, and stars without a name,
> With all the gardener Fancy e'er could feign,
> Who breeding flowers, will never breed the same:
> And there shall be for thee all soft delight
> That shadowy thought can win,
> A bright torch, and a casement ope at night,
> To let the warm Love in!

(50–67)

If the "Ode to Psyche" is about "mental life in the modern world," these
lines enact the process whereby the ancient fictions become subsumed under
the sovereignty of mental life. The space of antiquity becomes transformed
into inner landscapes of the mind, where classical allusions are lulled to

sleep and may perhaps never reawaken to breed the same. The "wreath'd trellis of a working brain" spins for itself arabesques of thought, as a way of enmeshing the elusive fictions of the past. Thus it seems misleading to propose that Psyche's name "recedes from the poem as her presence grows stronger there." Is it not, rather, that her name recedes because it is the presence of the poet's mind which grows stronger, at the expense, ironically, of the poem's founding fiction? The hovering Psyche is engulfed and all but extinguished in the recesses of the mind. It is as though the burden of the past depended for its alleviation on the modern poet clipping the wings of antiquity's fluttering fictions. The poet's inspiration signifies the expiration of Psyche.

Either as gardener or lepidopterist, then, the belated poet has to subdue his fiction in order to make it manageable; he seems to cheat Psyche into submission by recreating her in the privacy of his own mind. And Psyche's clipped wings recall Hazlitt's belief that "the progress of knowledge and refinement has a tendency to circumscribe the limits of the imagination, and to clip the wings of poetry." Thus the last stanza of the "Ode to Psyche" might be read as mapping, in brief, a history—the modern history of poetry, and the destiny of those fictions which had once made great poetry possible. At this point we should remember that both *Hyperion* and the odes were written during and after the time of Keats's regular attendance at Hazlitt's *Lectures on the English Poets*, at the Surrey Institution. In a sense, Hazlitt's *Lectures* trace the history of the decline and fall of poetry, the gradual and irreversible contraction of its once mighty empire of fictions. At the high beginning of this history stand Homer and Dante, Chaucer and Spenser, Shakespeare and Milton. At the end stands Wordsworth, the poet of mental life in the modern world. A poet like Milton, said Keats, "did not think into the human heart, as Wordsworth has done." But perhaps Wordsworth is "deeper than Milton" because "it has depended more upon the general and gregarious advance of intellect, than individual greatness of Mind." Hazlitt was well aware that the grand march of intellect did not guarantee a progress of poetry, as was Friedrich Schlegel, who contemplated the "fate and progress of poetry" as a tendency "to descend lower and lower" from its original "lofty flight—to approach nearer and nearer to the earth—till at last it sinks—never to rise again—into the common life and citizenship of ordinary men." The final sentences of Hazlitt's *Lectures on the English Poets* are reminiscent of Schlegel:

> I have thus gone through the task I intended, and have come at
> last to the level ground. I have felt my subject gradually sinking

from under me as I advanced, and have been afraid of ending in nothing. The interest has unavoidably decreased at almost every successive step of the progress, like a play that has its catastrophe in the first or second act.

The level ground of modern poetry was, in Hazlitt's view, occupied by Wordsworth, and it is significant that immediately before these concluding remarks he should quote a passage from "Intimations of Immortality"(179–90), which ends with a reference to "the philosophic mind." Wordsworth's poetry, said Hazlitt, is "not external, but internal; it does not depend upon tradition, or story, or old song; he furnishes it from his own mind, and is his own subject." This ambivalent judgement would already have been familiar to Keats, from Hazlitt's essay on *The Excursion* in *The Round Table*. Wordsworth "may be said to create his own materials; his thoughts are his real subject. . . . He lives in the busy solitude of his own heart; in the deep silence of thought." The point about the "Ode to Psyche" is that is suggests how the Wordsworthian mode might begin, of historical necessity, to replace more archaic modes of poetic discourse. As both classical fiction (a goddess to be worshipped) and emblem of soul or mind, Psyche might be said to situate the inevitable passage from "external" to "internal." It is however, characteristic of the ode that it should hover indeterminately, on the borders of fiction and mind, between the landscape of old song and the deep silence of thought. The poem ends, appropriately, with a threshold image. If the first stanza had projected the poet as a Cupid-figure, then the poem's final image, of "a casement ope at night / To let the warm Love in!," suggests a consummation about to happen. But here the poem ends. A felicitous union is anticipated rather than realized. The "embodiment" of Psyche remains problematic.

## III

"Ode on Grecian Urn": Leigh Hunt described the ode as a poem "on a sculptured vase," which is reminiscent of the eloquent image in *Endymion* of a "gold vase emboss'd / With long-forgotten story"(3, 126–27). Why does Hunt feel inclined to imagine Keats's poem as wrought upon something else? It may be that the poetic text itself is a parergonal trace which seeks to reinscribe itself on the silent, ineffable space of the absent image of the urn. In which case the poem is in some essential way both distanced and belated vis-à-vis the desired object of its attention.

The poet's difficulty in representing the object of his attention as an accomplished image is already suggested in the poem's opening lines:

> Thou still unravish'd bride of quietness,
>     Thou foster-child of silence and slow time,
>     Sylvan historian, who canst thus express
>     A flowery tale more sweetly than our rhyme.
>
>     (1–4)

A desire for empathy with the object yields a language that is rich, perhaps too rich. "In-feeling, in Keats," according to Hartman, "is always on the point of overidentifying." Might Keats already be in danger here of insisting too vehemently to bestow meaning on the urn, to exalt the object as signifier by overloading it with metaphor? David Simpson proposes that metaphor is "the natural mode of expression of a mind in a state of excitement, but this excitement can be radically distorting." As a "trope of desire," the ode's inaugural metaphor appears to distort and indeed to ravish the urn's inviolable alterity. Immediately we are in the thick of a dense cluster of metaphorical associations, layers of possible meanings that perhaps call too importunately for attention. As the poet himself confesses, his rhyme will be no "flowery tale," a floral verse that will flow undeviatingly, but will be an affair less "sweet," more harsh and burdensome. Lines 3 and 4 have been described by John Jones as "one of Keats's iceberg statements; the visible tip airs the vague and questionable commonplace that painting is, or can be, more eloquent than poetry; the rest . . . is immersed in his struggle with his chosen medium. Language is a discursive symbolism and takes time. Painting is not and does not." The poet "wants to write a Grecian Urn." Indeed the poet's iceberg statement already calls into question the overrepresented discursive symbolism of the opening two lines, thus anticipating the problematic stance of the poem as a whole. It may be that the urn is eloquent in a way that poetic discourse, even at its richest, can never be. Keats not only wants to write a Grecian urn but indeed *has* to write it—how else might this silent emblem of antiquity be summoned into significance? A problem, then, of expression: the poet will try to express, *press out*, a story (a narrative) from the urn's silent landscape.

We might read further, in order to surmise the fuller implications of the poem's overrepresented beginning:

> What leaf-fring'd legend haunts about thy shape
>     Of deities or mortals, or of both,
>         In Tempe or the dales of Arcady?
>     What men or gods are these? What maidens loth?
>     What mad pursuit? What struggle to escape?
>         What pipes and timbrels? What wild ecstasy?
>
>     (5–10)

Even as perfectly symmetrical a whole as the urn cannot, it seems, prevent a twofold parergonal deviation, a tendency towards arabesque hinted in the contrast between the perfection of the urn's imagined outline and the irregularity of the lines in the text itself. Not only is the legend "leaf-fring'd," but the long-forgotten story itself "haunts about" the urn's shape, like an apparition hovering restlessly without ever being able to settle. Considering that the whole poem can be read as a parergonal inscription over an absent, or at least never completely represented, object, the "flowery tale" at the urn's secret centre becomes displaced and "unwritten" as an array of partial images which refuse to organize themselves into a visibly coherent picture. The relation between the text, the urn's form, and its content or "legend," remains discontinuous and fragmentary, radically unaccomplished.

In a contemporary collection of vase engravings we read that

> the various beautiful borders which surround these designs, were not so placed in the original vases, but served there, merely to ornament the handles, and other parts, nor were the border and figures, which are upon the same Plate in this work, always upon the same vase. Nothing can exceed the different borders, in simplicity, in variety, in elegance, in richness, or in beauty, and all modern ornaments sink in the comparison.

Here the parergonal forms of antiquity are made to cohere in terms of "simplicity" and "elegance," against which "all modern ornaments sink in comparison." Is the Keatsian text, as a late ornament seeking to append itself to the monumental fiction of antiquity, in danger of sinking under the pressure of its own overrepresented discourse, and thus losing sight of its "object" altogether? "The embellishments of a Vase, or of an Urn," observed Archibald Alison, "are beautiful, both from the dimunition of their size, and from the delicacy of their workmanship." But there is nothing delicately diminutive about the fragmented images constituting the urn's "leaf-fring'd legend." Rather they threaten to warp the urn's frame, to unfix the relation between content and form.

"To put a statue into motion," observed Hazlitt, "or to give appropriate, natural, and powerful expression to set features of any kind, is at all times difficult." But Hazlitt's caveat is ignored as the poet worries the urn with a series of importunate questions. As Hartman point out, however, the figures on the urn "resist the explainer-ravisher"; the effect of the poet's "crescendoing questions" is that "their very intensity of speculation seems to animate the urn until its mystery is in danger of being dissolved, its form broken for the sake of a message." In fact the form does not break, and any "message" emerges as a repetition of fragmentary images, unanswered questions that refuse to compose into a semblance of narrative within the urn's frame. The story lacks "intelligible sequence." In the face of a perpetual ambivalence generated by the repetition of "What" and "or" (proposing alternatives that come to nothing), the urn represents not a pageant or legend but rather unidentifiable fragments of a vision, amounting to so many intractable refusals to speak and to define. And might not the surmise of a "mad pursuit" and "wild ecstasy" indirectly and ironically refer to the poet's own activity? As an explainer-ravisher, he himself is engaged in a mad pursuit of a recalcitrant object, as he endeavours to redeem this emblem of his supreme fiction from silence. Returning to the poem's opening lines, we may clarify some of the metaphorical associations by surmising that it is the poet himself who assumes the role of the aggressive bridegroom-lover, as he tries to coax or indeed to violate the image out of quietness into significant discourse. The rest of the poem turns on the implied disharmony between the urn's silence and the poet's music loud and long, between the "slow time" of an irretrievable past and the more agitated tempo of the poet's questionings.

Thus Keats's romance with antiquity threatens to take a somewhat violent turn, as the poet turns the urn in a desire to make it speak its eloquent but withheld narrative. He want to write a Grecian urn, or else we might say that he endeavours to *read* the urn out of silence. But the poet finds himself deprived of the confidence of a scholar like Henry Moses, who could write on the subject of antique vases with enviable assurance: "Few remains of antiquity have excited more interest than vases. . . . By attentively studying the stories they record, the scholar has been enabled to throw much light upon the mythology, the history, the manners and customs of the ancients." On the contrary, the more attentively does the poet seem to study the urn's "leaf-fring'd legend," the more opaque becomes its content. "The spatial, so-called plastic work of art," writes Derrida, "does not necessarily prescribe an order of reading. I can place myself in front of it, begin with the top or bottom, at times move around." Moses solves this problem by supplementing his account of the celebrated Portland Vase with two pictorial images, one of which is a view of "that side of the vase which all who have set about to explain or describe the objects represented seem to have agreed in regarding as the first compartment," while the second is an impression of the vase's images flattened out, as it were, into a simple linear, two-dimensional surface. The first image, which can of course only represent part of the object, seeks to do justice to the vase's proper shape and dimension, while the second image facilitates the writer's reading of the vase's story. But one of the problems facing the poet in the

"Ode on a Grecian Urn" is that he does not quite know where or how to begin his reading of the urn's legend, which steadfastly refuses to be flattened out into an intelligible narrative sequence.

This lack of a proper mode of reading produces a certain bewilderment, a trace of which we can also find in the "Ode on Indolence":

> They pass'd, like figures on a marble urn,
>     When shifted round to see the other side;
>         They came again; as when the urn once more
> Is shifted round, the first seen shades return;
>     And they were strange to me, as may betide
>         With vases, to one deep in Phidian lore.
>
> (5–10)

Or rather we should say that the strangeness registered in the "Ode on Indolence" does not become disconcerting for the poet, as is the case in the "Ode on a Grecian Urn." Indeed, the mood which reigns in the "Ode on Indolence" seems precisely opposite to that which we find in the "Ode on a Grecian Urn," where all is restlessness, desire and disappointment. At a famous moment in one of the letter-journals to his brother and sister-in-law, Keats says: "Neither Poetry, nor Ambition, nor Love have any alertness of countenance as they pass by me: they seem rather like three figures on a greek vase—a Man and two women—whom no one but myself could distinguish in their disguisement." In his state of happy indolence, the poet refuses to be moved by the blandishments of these "figures" which represent, one supposes, the most pressing concerns of Keats's life. And he remains unmoved because although he is able to identify each figure, in his state of indolence he prefers to watch them "fade" (to borrow an important word from the "Ode on Indolence") into indistinctness, and thus be spared the gaze of their alert countenance. Hence the pervasive imagery of hovering indistinctness in the "Ode on Indolence": the figures on the marble urn are evoked as "shades"(8), "shadows . . . muffled in so hush a masque"(11–12), "ghosts"(51), and "phantoms"(59). For a brief moment the poet thinks of rousing himself and following the beckoning figures, as though they were real forces to be reckoned with. But he lapses back into his mood of indolent revery, while Poesy, Love and Ambition fade once again into "masque-like figures on the dreamy urn"(56).

In the "Ode on a Grecian Urn," of course, the urn is anything but "dreamy," as the poet desires to take the "masque" for real (to unveil the imagined reality behind the mask), to bring the shadowy into distinctness. As I have suggested, the strangeness remarked by the poet in the "Ode on

Indolence" now becomes disconcerting, as we can see in the extended oxymoron at the beginning of the second stanza:

> Heard melodies are sweet, but those unheard
> Are sweeter, therefore, ye soft pipes, play on;
> Not to the sensual ear, but, more endear'd,
> Pipe to the spirit ditties of no tone.
>
> (11–14)

These lines, I suspect, tease the reader as much as the urn teases the poet. Their exquisite cadences scarcely conceal the possibility that the poet un-ashamedly *pretends* to overhear the silent discourse of antiquity. Hazlitt noted that the ear is "oftener courted by silence than noise; and the sounds that break that silence sink deeper and more durably into the mind." But the only noise that will break the urn's silence is the poem's plangent rhetoric. The "play" of the soft pipes is precisely this, a tease, an irony, a playing on or with the poet's apparently nostalgic susceptibilities. Might not the overt pun, in the assonance of "ear" / "endear'd," briefly hint at the impossibility of ever believing in the paradox of the "spirit" rehearsing unheard melodies?

Our reading of the Keatsian text comprehends two different though obviously related levels of discourse: the narrative *manqué* situated on the urn, and the narrative of the poet's desire to read that narrative. Perhaps the elusiveness of the one testifies to the difficulty of the other. Indeed, the "leaf-fring'd legend," far from being legible or translatable, begins to signify a profound rift between the poet and his supreme fiction: haunting about the shape of the urn, it hovers free-floatingly in middle air, in a space which is a vacancy or lack. Once again the frame (and what more promising a frame than the shaped and delimited surface of a vase?) appears unable to contain the long-forgotten story of antiquity. In these following lines, the frame's invaginated structure is exposed, as the text's syntactic sheen be-comes punctuated by gaps and pauses, intimating crevices and cracks in the image:

> Fair youth, beneath the trees, thou canst not leave
> Thy song, nor ever can those trees be bare;
> Bold lover, never, never canst thou kiss,
> Though winning near the goal—yet, do not grieve;
> She cannot fade, though thou hast not thy bliss,
> For ever wilt thou love, and she be fair!
>
> (15–20)

The rhythm falters and hesitates. It is as though the poem's rhetoric, burdened as it is by a long series of qualified negatives, were on the point of disintegrating, fragmenting its narrative endeavour and uncovering the inarticulate space between. We might continue the argument from the previous stanza and suggest that these lines express an oblique commentary on the poet's own condition. Has not the poet dared to approach the urn in the guise of a bold lover, bold to the extent of appearing a ravisher? Yet his romance with antiquity can never be consummated, it can only ever be a liminal affair. We might go further and interpret these lines as a virtual allegory of the poet's belatedness (which is, after all, the condition of his romance with antiquity). "Fair youth, beneath the trees, thou canst not leave / Thy song, nor ever can those trees be bare": consider for a moment "leave" not in the sense of "abandon," but as echoing "leaf-fring'd legend." To "leave" is to surround or decorate with leaves.

"If Poetry comes not as naturally as the Leaves to a tree it had better not come at all." Keats's figure to express the natural flowering of poetry is not wholly unrelated to the image of the "leaf-fring'd legend," insofar as both harbour the notion of embellishment. But the relation becomes problematic when we read: "nor ever can those trees be bare." Symbolizing, perhaps, the abundance and fertility of the imagination's founding fictions, the trees in the "Ode on a Grecian Urn" are in some essential way beyond the reach of the belated poet. He cannot embellish his song (and thus celebrate the natural fertility of Poesy) in the way that the ancient artist could "fringe" his legend. John Ruskin had this to say on the parergonality of flowers and leaves:

> Wherever men exist in a perfectly civilized and healthy state, they have vegetation around them; wherever their state approaches that of innocence or perfectness, it approaches that of Paradise,—it is a dressing of garden. And, therefore, where nothing else can be used for ornament, vegetation may; vegetation in any form, however fragmentary, however abstracted. A single leaf laid upon the angle of a stone, or the mere form or framework of the leaf drawn upon it, or the mere shadow and ghost of the leaf . . . possesses a charm which nothing else can replace; a charm not exciting, nor demanding laborious thought or sympathy, but perfectly simple, peaceful, and satisfying.

In this version of the Golden Age, foliage acquires an almost sacred status. Milton's Adam and Eve likewise spend their time before the Fall tending flowers in the Garden of Eden. But in a burdened and belated culture, even this fundamental type of parergon is denied to the poet. As Herder lamented: "When Homer had sung, no second Homer in the same path could be conceived: he plucked the flower of the epic garland, and all who followed must content themselves with a few leaves." Ruskin himself used the same imagery as a metaphor to express his own version of decline and belatedness: he observed how

> the human mind, in its acceptance of this feature of ornament, proceeded from the ground, and followed as it were, the natural growth of the tree. It began with the rude and solid trunk . . . then the branches shot out, and became loaded with leaves; autumn came, the leaves were shed, and the eye was directed to the extremities of the delicate branches;—the Renaissance frosts came, and all perished.

So perhaps Keats's floral language, in the odes but also in the earlier verse, is a necessity rather than a luxury, the symptom of a desire to prolong contact with a world (a landscape of fictions) which has virtually disappeared but which seems to be indispensable to the flowering of Poesy. Otherwise the modern poet might be left with nothing but some "skreaking and skrittering residuum" of language (Stevens); he is a gatecrasher at some divine *fête champêtre*, condemned to pick up the litter: "For empty shells were scattered on the grass, / And grape stalks but half bare, and remnants more" (*The Fall of Hyperion*, 1, 32–33). And the poet will eat deliciously only to fall again, another Adam: "down I sunk / Like a Silenus on an antique vase"(1, 55–56). Whichever way he turns, the belated poet is tempted with forbidden fruit. The remnants of the banquet on which the poet stumbles in *The Fall of Hyperion* might still be "Sweet smelling"(1, 34), just as the urn's tuneless ditties might be "sweeter than heard melodies"; but there is always a danger that the flowers of speech garlanded by the modern poet will be malodorous ones.

## IV

There is no main verb in the incantatory rhetoric of the ode's third stanza—as though any sense of temporal movement were to be elided. Perhaps the poet's invocations are intended to focus the urn's long-forgotten story more intensely, to magnify its impression on the mind:

> Ah, happy, happy boughs! that cannot shed
> Your leaves, nor ever bid the spring adieu;

And, happy melodist, unwearied,
   For ever piping songs for ever new;
More happy love! more happy, happy love!
   For ever warm and still to be enjoy'd,
     For ever panting, and for ever young;
All breathing human passion far above,
   That leaves a heart high-sorrowful and cloy'd,
     A burning forehead, and a parching tongue.
                         (21–30)

But once again language threatens to overrepresent the scene. Images from the previous stanza recur and seem to be required to perform more feats of signification than in fact they are able to do (even the ironic assonance of "ear," / "endear'd" is repeated in "unwearied"). Certain phrases, notably "happy" and "for ever," are repeated until they become virtually meaningless; they suffocate, and are suffocated by, the immediate context. Again we witness the text's rhetoric tending to violate the urn's silent alterity. Overburdened by the importunate discursiveness of language, the urn is in danger of being effaced, or else of dividing and breaking under the strain: overrepresentation threatens fracture and fragmentation.

Given the inability of the poet's discourse to reanimate the urn's silent story, the contrast intended by the stanza's final three lines would seem to be ironically misleading. The poet strives to redeem the urn according to the language of sensuous life: "For ever warm and still to be enjoy'd / For ever panting, and for ever young." But these overtly "human" terms serve merely to divert us briefly away from the essential inhumanity of the urn's figures. To borrow a suggestive phrase from Hazlitt, we might say that the urn's legend wants *gusto*: "It has not the internal character, the living principle in it. It is a smooth surface, not a warm, moving mass." This feeling becomes more explicit, of course, with the references to "marble men and maidens" and "Cold Pastoral" in the ode's concluding stanza. The whole poem moves towards a recognition of the irreversible alterity of Greece, the inhumanity and (in)difference of the past. "What modern," lamented Hazlitt, "can enter fully into the spirit of the ancient Greek mythology, or rival the symmetry of its naked forms?" There is a significant passage in the first of the *Lectures on the English Poets* which might have impressed Keats. "The Greek statues," Hazlitt argues,

> are little else than specious forms. They are marble to the touch
> and to the heart. They have not an informing principle within
> them. In their faultless excellence they appear sufficient to them-

selves. By their beauty they are raised above the frailties of passion or suffering. By their beauty they are deified. But they are not objects of religious faith to us, and their forms are a reproach to common humanity. They seem to have no sympathy with us, and not to want our admiration.

I take these sentences as beautifully apt to the experience of the "Ode on a Grecian Urn." Antiquity, it seems, will always scorn the modern poet's advances. In which case the repetition of "for ever," instead of yielding intimations of immortality (a perpetuity of some ideal plenitude), betrays rather a changeless state of unrealized humanity, a sterile rhetoric of consolation. In the face of this bleak surmise of a *perpetuum immobile*, it may be, then, that "breathing human passion" offers a possibility of release, a descent from the heady but unsympathetic realm of antiquity ("far above") to the guarantee of a more authentic reality ("on earth"). Frank Kermode has proposed that "the assurance [of] a timeless and motionless transcendent world reduces to insignificance the *faits divers* which seem to constitute the narrative of ordinary life." But perhaps it is the incidental detail of ordinary life (the scandalous presence of burning foreheads and parching tongues) which will constitute for the belated poet a more genuine narrative than the long-forgotten story of antiquity.

We might read the ambivalent implications of the stanza's concluding lines from another point of view. Without subscribing to the rather ambitious claim that the *Anatomy of Melancholy* "provided Keats with hints for the main theme and much of the general philosophy" in the "Ode on a Grecian Urn," we may nevertheless appeal to Burton's text for a possible gloss on the poem. Burton writes that "pleasant objects are infinite, whether they be such as have life, or be without life." He goes on to say that "these things in themselves are pleasing and good, singular ornaments, necessary, comely, and fit to be had; but when we fix an immoderate eye, and dote on them over much, this pleasure may turn to pain, bring much sorrow and discontent unto us, work our final overthrow, and cause melancholy in the end." Are not the discontent and melancholy which break through at the end of the third stanza a consequence of the poet's "immoderate eye" desiring to focus too intensely on its object? In its rage for identification the poet's overrepresented discourse violates the decorum of the image as pleasant object and will indeed cause the heart to be left "high-sorrowful." A comment from one of Keats's older contemporaries affords an illuminating contrast. According to Dugald Stewart, "the Beauty of the object increases in proportion to the rapture with which we gaze on it." This, perhaps, is the kind of simplified feeling that a lesser poem might have been content to celebrate; but there is no room for nostalgic exaltations of Beauty in the "Ode on a Grecian Urn." Burton's psychology is much the more astute, and more appropriate to the Keatsian text. If the poet gazes with rapture on the urn, it is not so much the urn's "beauty" but rather its intransigence and indifference which make themselves felt: rapture turns into melancholy.

In the poem's middle stanzas, then, the ambiguity of the urn's presence seems to be felt most keenly. With the fourth stanza the focus shifts, promising another perspective:

> Who are these coming to the sacrifice?
>     To what green altar, O mysterious priest,
> Lead'st thou that heifer lowing at the skies,
>     And all her silken flanks with garlands drest?
> What little town by river or sea shore,
>     Or mountain-built with peaceful citadel,
>         Is emptied of this folk, this pious morn?
> And, little town, thy streets for evermore
>     Will silent be; and not a soul to tell
>         Why thou art desolate, can e'er return.
>
>                                         (31–40)

What is, I think, remarkable about this stanza is that the details seem to emerge, as it were, from nowhere. The fact that there is little or no relation between this new scene and the previous stanza begins to confirm a suspicion that the poem, like the legend which it desires to recuperate, comprises a succession of discontinuous parts: the text is barely redeemable as a whole. It may be, then, that the form of the ode itself is given to internal fragmentation. Hugh Blair referred to the ode as the most ancient poetic form, close to music: "Hence, that neglect of regularity, those digressions, and that disorder which it is supposed to admit." More recently, Thomas McFarland has proposed that "in no other vehicle available to the poet is the tension between fragmentation and wholeness so much the very essence of the form as it is with the ode. This statement is, I think, amply borne out by the fourth stanza of the "Ode on a Grecian Urn." A narrative with intelligible sequence (a picture with a frame) is sought, but we are given only brief surmises, fragments of perception. The urn, it seems, only acquires existence as it is produced in the very act of the poem's composition. Or rather the image threatens to disappear in the folds of what Keats calls "innumerable compositions and decompositions," creations and destroyings on the level of discourse which tend to displace indefinitely the urn's stable presence as an accomplished object. The urn enters the text with difficulty, fragmentarily, as a vague and shadowy form. Perhaps the fourth stanza tries to dress the urn's "meagre outline" with, in Hazlitt's words, "colouring" and "adventitious ornament." But these images seem unable to transcend their own arbitrary status within the poem; they are adventitious and nothing more. Since they possess "no narratively defined origin or terminus," it is impossible to discover where they come from, how they might be organized, what they mean.

To put it another way, we could say that the fourth stanza is packed with signifiers which refuse to signify. In this sense, the poetic outline of the Grecian Urn is very different from Thomas Kirk's outlines from the figures and compositions on William Hamilton's vases. In Kirk's book, each plate, like the plate of the Portland Vase in the Moses volume, is a scene flattened out to represent the composition on a particular vase. And each detail in a plate is made to *signify*. Here, for example, is the account of one particular plate:

> That this is a *representation* of a feast of Venus, is *discernible* by the dove, with the fillet placed near it, as well as by the branches of myrtle and the pearl girdles, which the goddess and her priestesses wear. Two *symbols* are placed on the *symbolic* pillar of Bacchus; one is a pine apple, *indicative* of that god as well as of Cybele, the other may probably be the *bœtilus* in shape of a small urn, which *denotes* Venus; the armed figure *signifies* the god of war, whose connexion with the goddess, to whom this feast is consecrated, needs no explanation; she was often *represented* in armour, particularly, according to Pausanias, in her temples at Lacedemon and Corinth; *several gems corroborate this testimony.*
>
> (italics mine)

By making details signify in this way the reader attains a complete mastery over the sign; the emblems of antiquity become perfectly legible. The text to another plate begins thus: "Whenever a female was *represented* sitting upon a stool, it was always a *mark* of dignity among the ancients, and when to this was joined the *patera*, or bowl, held near the head, it became a *sign* of some divinity. *By these marks we may know*, that this painting *represents* Ceres, with two of her initiated priestesses near her" (italics mine)—and the account ends with a satisfied acknowledgment that "the whole forms a composition at once simple and beautiful." But the Grecian urn possesses no lucid signifying marks, and its long-forgotten story withdraws at the very moment when it seems to promise to make itself heard in the text. Thus the images which intrude in the fourth stanza barely function as images at all, since they refuse to form a composition that is intelligible, let alone simple and beautiful. They are, rather, signifiers of a lack, an absence around which the poem's language as it were tissues itself. The desired narrative remains stillborn, on the threshold of presence yet imprisoned within a twilight zone bordering on presence and absence, silence and meaning. Keats might have been familiar with Hazlitt's definition of art as "the microscope of the mind," which "converts every object into a little universe in itself." This is, perhaps, what the ode in its middle stanzas attempts yet fails to do with the urn—not merely to apprehend the image as a silent form but to convert it into intelligible *content*, to give it significant dimension ("a little universe") where consciousness might secure a vantage point for itself. Instead, however, the modern poet's art, like the little town, is "desolate," so late that it can no longer rehearse the ancient fictions which embellish the urn.

## V

The urn maps a landscape of absence, of vacancy, the O at the centre of "desolate." And the poem's fifth stanza begins and ends with the sound of this tuneless number ("O "/ "know"):

> O Attic shape! Fair attitude! with brede
>    Of marble men and maidens overwrought,
> With forest branches and the trodden weed;
>    Thou, silent form, dost tease us out of thought,
> As doth eternity: Cold Pastoral!
>    When old age shall this generation waste,
>       Thou shalt remain, in midst of other woe
>    Than ours, a friend to man, to whom thou say'st,
> "Beauty is truth, truth beauty,"—that is all
>       Ye know on earth, and all ye need to know,
>                                            (41–50)

At least one critic has commented on the "lurching" assonance of "O Attic shape! Fair attitude!." Perhaps the overwrought diction is meant to compensate for the initial "O." For the urn's shape (the shape, implicitly, of Keats's supreme fiction) would seem to be precisely this, an O, a cipher, not a rounded whole but a rounded hole, a frame without a middle, a form deprived of content. This initial O is a perfect sign of antiquity's silence, its problematic and devious presence within the modern text. The emblem invites the poet to gaze at it as through a frame, but all he glimpses are fragments or traces of a long-forgotten story which defies adequate recuperation.

The last stanza of the "Ode on a Grecian Urn" begins with an intimation of endings. O is an omega, and immediately collides with its opposite, the capital A in "Attic." A is for Antiquity, the original site of creative beginnings, to which the modern omega-poet is compelled to return. Thus O and A comprehend the destiny of Keats's supreme fiction, whose beginning and end dissolve in the vacant space of the urn's frame. The poet as the letter O: a framer without a story, he finds himself at the opposite end of that mythic time whose beginning is signified by the supreme moment of Antiquity. As a belated greeting to the beautiful mythology of Greece, the "Ode on a Grecian Urn," is indeed an odeon where the melodies of ancient music have long since ceased to be heard; all that remain are "ditties of no tone."

"With brede / Of marble men and maidens overwrought." We recall the image, in the first stanza, of the legend haunting about the shape of the urn. "Overwrought" suggests both "overrepresented" and "superimposed"—reaffirming a suspicion that there might indeed be something adventitious in the legend's parergonal relation to the silent form over which it hovers. And is not this indeterminacy repeated in the activity of the poet himself, as he tries vainly to bring his discourse into alignment with the urn's narrative? In which case there is a further implication that the urn has been "overwrought" by the text itself, by the violence of its desire to frame. This is the nature of the poem's active ravishment, that it violates the urn's silent form, seeking to tie it down, enmeshing it in the arborescent arabesques ("forest branches" and "trodden weed") of discourse.

The images forming the "brede" confirm the impossibility of the urn's story ever emerging as a legible sign since they are imprisoned on the edge of the frame, overwrought upon a nought, the O of an outline. We can trace the images of "forest branches" and "trodden weed" back to the presence of trees and foliage in stanzas two and three, and to the "flowery tale" in the first stanza. But Keats's floral language now seems to be flowing into an impasse, where the poverty implied in "trodden weed" quietly mocks the endeavour to recuperate the urn's "leaf-fring'd legend." It may be that the text, like *Hyperion*, has overwrought itself in trying to monumentalize something which can only ever be rewritten as parergonal trace, as a pale, marginal gloss that weaves itself elusively around an absent centre.

The poet is left teased and thoughtless before the urn, which seems as inconceivable as "eternity" (the urn, as a vocality, drifts down and loses itself in the ungraspable, inaudible sound-space of eternity). Hence the violent interruption of rebuke and outrage: "Cold Pastoral!" "Cold" emphasizes the feeling of inhumanity already registered by the urn's "marble" legend. In fact the phrase is an oxymoron. We scarcely need the testimony of the "Ode to a Nightingale" to surmise that for Keats pastoral is replete with imaginings of "sunburnt mirth" and "the warm South." Pastoral, we might say, supposes a vision of antiquity instinct with life, animated and warm. So why, in the last stanza of the "Ode on a Grecian Urn," has Keats's version of pastoral gone cold? I suggest that this late utterance intervenes as a counterstatement to the earlier, more benign and hopeful invocation of the urn as a "Sylvan historian." "Sylvan" belongs to the conventional rhetoric of pastoral: at this stage the poet thinks of the urn as a purveyor of Theocritean idylls, flower tales which narrate the text of antiquity in it happiest guise. But this initial response comes to be revised and displaced during the course of the poem, reaching a climax in "Cold Pastoral!" Marble to the touch and to the heart, the urn's legend chills the poem's atmosphere; in vain does the poet try to bring life back into the frieze ("For ever warm"). From the notion of the urn as a simple story-teller ("historian") the poet has moved to a bleaker recognition of the demise of antiquity's leaf-fringed legends. Such narratives remain cold and indifferent to the modern poet; they are pastimes which can no longer be adequately represented.

There is, I think, an important break in continuity, an ironic swerve, between the first and second halves of the ode's last stanza. Or rather, the tone of rebuke betrayed in "Cold Pastoral!" seems deflected, yet it persists, hovering and more muted, in an unexpected way:

> When old age shall this generation waste,
>     Thou shalt remain, in midst of other woe
> Than ours, a friend to man, to whom thou say'st,
>     "Beauty is truth, truth beauty,"—that is all
>         Ye know on earth, and all ye need to know.
>
> (46–50)

Critics have been and no doubt always will be perplexed by "Beauty is truth, truth beauty." But how are we to read the rest of this concluding sentence, of which, after all, the poem's famous dictum is only a part? I would argue that these final cadences, sententious in diction and in tone, articulate a fine and appropriate irony in the poet's response to his dialogue manqué with the urn. Hartman is right to observe that "the Grecian urn's 'Beauty is Truth, Truth Beauty' remains an extroverted, lapidary cry. However appropriate its philosophy, its form is barely snatched from a defeat of the imagination." Teased and defeated by the urn's silence, the poet adopts the rhetorical pose of a moralist; he becomes a composer of epitaphs which are eloquent yet meaningless. But within the ironic framework of the whole sentence, Keats's lapidary statement is appropriate neither as form nor as philosophy. Or rather, it is appropriate only insofar as it helps to register the irony of the whole utterance.

In other words, the poet takes his revenge on the urn by moralizing it, by forcing it to speak a "sublime commonplace." The irony of this gesture is missed by a certain kind of nostalgic criticism which interprets the poem's ending as a celebration of art's universality and permanence: "The *archeological* message of the urn is dead, its *aesthetic* message is alive 'for ever.' " Far from being a genuine "friend to man," offering consolations of truth and beauty, the urn remains sublimely indifferent to the scandal of mortality, the wasting of generations where youth "grows pale, and spectre-thin, and dies" ("Ode to a Nightingale"). Hence the ambivalence of the poem's epitaph. According to Wordsworth, the "first requisite" of an epitaph is that "it should speak, in a tone which shall sink into the heart, the general language of humanity as connected with the subject of death." This is, perhaps, the duplicity of Keats's supreme fiction: inviting the belated poet's active engagement, it nevertheless refuses to humanize itself, and speaks instead the unmediated language of death.

At the last, then, Keats's text turns ironically into an urn-burial. If an epitaph "presupposes a Monument, upon which it is to be engraven," then the poem's final lines, including "Beauty is truth, truth beauty," engrave themselves on a tomb-text, as a late parergon to that which has already passed away in the phrase "Cold Pastoral!" We are told that

> the Etruscans, the Greeks, and the Romans, followed two different methods with respect to their dead; some they burnt, others they buried. The ashes of the former were carried from the funeral pile and put into vases, which were commonly placed in niches, made in the walls of the sepulchral apartments. The higher classes had their ashes put into marble urns highly sculptured.

No matter how ornate and embellished the urn appears, it cannot defraud the reality of death. "Truth with beauty," remarked Hazlitt, "suggests the feeling of immortality." But the ode's equation of truth and beauty implies a feeling of immortality which is deeply ambiguous, since it cannot evade the modern poet's inability ever to reawaken the urn's dormant narrative. The "Ode on a Grecian Urn" speaks the historicity of art, and its melancholy yet inevitable connection with the subject of death.

# Chronology

1795    John Keats is born October 31, at 24 Moorfields Pavement Row, London.

1803    Sent to Clarke School at Enfield.

1804    Keats's father falls off a horse and dies.

1810    Keats's mother dies; his grandmother, Alice Jennings, sets up a trust fund for the Keats children.

1811    Keats removed from school and apprenticed to Thomas Hammond, an apothecary and surgeon in Edmonton, north of London.

1814    Keats writes his first poems at age 18 or 19.

1816    First published work in May; journeys to Margate on the coast to write; returns to London and meets Leigh Hunt and Benjamin Robert Haydon; writes sonnet on Chapman's *Homer* in October.

1817    First volume appears in March. Keats begins *Endymion;* visits Benjamin Bailey at Oxford; finishes *Endymion* in November. Writes "Negative Capability" letter, and sees Wordsworth, Lamb, and others at Haydon's "Immortal Dinner."

1818    Reconsiders his entire career from January to June. Writes new Shakespearean sonnets, and writes "Isabella" (March and April). Visits ill brother Tom (March to early May); returns to London; walking tour of northern England with Charles Brown; returns to find his brother in worsened condition. Angry reviews of *Endymion*. Begins *Hyperion* (September), nursing Tom until he dies (December 1). Meets Fanny Brawne (November). Keats rents his rooms from Charles Brown in Wentworth Place, Hampstead.

1819    From January to February writes "The Eve of St. Agnes" at Chichester and Bedhampton. Returns to Hampstead, writes "The Eve of St. Mark." Meets Coleridge in April; the Brawnes move next door; writes "Vale of Soul-Making" letter, "La Belle Dame sans Merci," and "Ode to Psyche." Writes odes—Nightingale, Grecian Urn, Melancholy, and Indolence, in May. From June until August: on Isle of Wight, with Charles Brown; writes first half of "Lamia," and part of *The Fall of Hyperion;* begins writing love letters to Fanny Brawne. Writes "Otho the Great" with Brown. In September finishes "Lamia," gives up on *The Fall of Hyperion;* writes ode "To Autumn," and returns to London. Becomes ill in October. Begins engagement with Fanny Brawne; writes Fragment of "King Stephen," and "The Cap and Bells."

1820    In February Keats, now gravely ill with tuberculosis, has a hemorrhage and remains confined for months. Moves (May–August) to Kentish Town, when Brown rents his house to others. Third book is published—*Lamia, Isabella, The Eve of St. Agnes, and other Poems.* On September 18 he sails for Italy with Joseph Severn, arriving at Naples on October 31. In Rome, he finds rooms in 26 Piazza di Spagna (now the Keats–Shelley Memorial House).

1821    Dies on February 23. Buried in the Protestant cemetery in Rome.

# Contributors

HAROLD BLOOM, Sterling Professor of the Humanities at Yale University, is the author of *The Anxiety of Influence, Poetry and Repression,* and many other volumes of literary criticism. His forthcoming study, *Freud: Transference and Authority,* attempts a full-scale reading of all of Freud's major writings. A MacArthur Prize Fellow, he is general editor of five series of literary criticism published by Chelsea House.

WALTER JACKSON BATE is University Professor of English at Harvard. He is renowned for his critical biographies of Dr. Johnson and Keats.

MORRIS DICKSTEIN is Professor of English at Queens College and the author of *Gates of Eden.*

GEOFFREY H. HARTMAN is Professor of Comparative Literature at Yale. He is best known for his writings on Wordsworth, and for his work in critical theory, including *Beyond Formalism, Criticism in the Wilderness,* and *Saving the Text.*

STUART A. ENDE is Professor of English at the California Institute of Technology and the author of *Keats and the Sublime.*

LESLIE BRISMAN, Professor of English at Yale, is the author of *Milton's Poetry of Choice and Its Romantic Heirs.*

PAUL H. FRY is Associate Professor of English at Yale. His books include *The Poet's Calling in the English Ode* and *The Reach of Criticism: Method and Perception in Literary Theory.*

HELEN VENDLER, Professor of English at Boston University and at Harvard, is widely known for her books on Yeats and Stevens, as well as her book on contemporary poetry, *Part of Nature, Part of Us.*

MARTIN ASKE teaches in the Department of English Studies and Comparative Literature at the University of Hong Kong.

# Bibliography

Allott, Miriam, ed. *The Poems of John Keats*. New York: Norton, 1970.

Barnard, John, "Keats's Tactile Vision: 'Ode to Psyche' and the Early Poetry." *Keats-Shelley Memorial Bulletin* 33 (1982): 1–24.

Bate, Walter Jackson. *John Keats*. Cambridge: Harvard University Press, 1963.

Bloom, Harold, ed. *Modern Critical Views: John Keats*. New York: Chelsea House, 1985.

Bowra, C. M. " 'Ode on a Grecian Urn.' " In *The Romantic Imagination*. Cambridge: Harvard University Press, 1949.

Brooks, Cleanth, "History without Footnotes: An Account of Keats's Urn." *The Sewanee Review* 52 (1944): 89–101.

Brown, Homer. "Creations and Destroyings: Keats's Protestant Hymn, the 'Ode to Psyche.' " *Diacritics* 6 (1970): 49–50.

Burke, Kenneth. "Symbolic Action in a Poem by Keats." *Accent* 4 (1943): 30–42.

Bush, Douglas. *John Keats: His Life and Writings*. New York: Macmillan, 1966.

De Man, Paul, ed. *The Selected Poetry of Keats*. New York: Signet, 1966.

Dickstein, Morris. *Keats and His Poetry: A Study in Development*. Chicago: The University of Chicago Press, 1971.

Ende, Stuart A. *Keats and the Sublime*. New Haven: Yale University Press, 1976.

Evert, Walter H. *Aesthetic Myth in the Poetry of Keats*. Princeton: Princeton University Press, 1965.

Fogle, Richard Harter. *The Imagery of Keats and Shelley*. Hamden, Conn.: Archon, 1962.

Ford, Newell F. *The Prefigurative Imagination of John Keats*. Palo Alto, Calif.: Stanford University Press, 1951.

Gradman, Barry. *Metamorphosis in Keats*. New York: New York University Press, 1980.

Gurney, Stephen. " 'Finite Transcendence' in Keats's 'Ode to a Nightingale': A Heideggerian Reading." *Soundings* 66, no. 1 (1983): 46–69.

Halpern, Sheldon. "Time and Tempo in Keats's 'Ode on a Grecian Urn.' " *Language and Style: An International Journal* 16, no. 2 (1983): 169–86.

Harrison, Thomas P. "Keats and a Nightingale." *English Studies* 41 (1960): 353–59.

Hartman, Geoffrey H. "Reading Aright: Keats's 'Ode to Psyche.' " In *Center and Labyrinth: Essays in Honor of Northrop Frye,* edited by Eleanor Cook, Chaviva

Hosek, Jay Macpherson, Patricia Parker. Toronto: University of Toronto Press, 1983.

Hirst, Wolf Z. *John Keats*. Boston: Twayne, 1981.

Holloway, John. "The Odes of Keats." In *The Charted Mirror*. London: Routledge & Kegan Paul, 1960.

Lau, Beth. "Keats, Associationism, and 'Ode to a Nightingale.' " *Keats–Shelley Journal* 32 (1983): 46–62.

Levine, George R. "The Arrogance of Keats's Grecian Urn." *Essays in Literature* 10, no. 1 (1983): 39–44.

Lyon, Harvey T. *Keats's Well-Read Urn*. New York: Holt, Rinehart & Winston, 1958.

McLuhan, Herbert Marshall. "Aesthetic Pattern in Keats's Odes." *University of Toronto Quarterly* 12 (1943): 167–79.

Meanes, Russell. "Keats and the 'Impersonal' Therapist: Notes on Empathy and the Therapeutic Screen." *Psychiatry* 46 (1983): 73–82.

Miller, Bruce. "Does Critical Consensus Exist? The Case of Keats's Nightingale Ode." *Research Studies* 50, no. 3/4 (1982): 133–42.

Murry, John Middleton. *Keats*. London: Jonathan Cape, 1955.

Perkins, David. "Keats's Odes and Letters: Recurrent Diction and Imagery." *Keats–Shelly Journal* 2 (1953): 51–60.

Pollard, David. *The Poetry of Keats: Language and Experience*. Totowa, N.J.: Barnes & Noble, 1984.

Pope, Deborah. "The Dark Side of the Urn: A Re-Evaluation of the Speaker in 'Ode on a Grecian Urn.' " *Essays in Literature* 10, no. 1 (1983): 45–63.

Rhodes, Jack Wright, comp. *Keats's Major Odes: An Annotated Bibliography of the Criticism*. Westport, Conn.: Greenwood, 1984.

Shackford, Martha Hale. "The 'Ode on a Grecian Urn.' " *Keats–Shelley Journal* 4 (1955): 51–60.

Sharp, Ronald. *Keats, Skepticism, and the Religion of Beauty*. Athens: University of Georgia Press, 1979.

Southam, B. C. "The Ode 'To Autumn.' " *Keats–Shelley Journal* 9 (1960): 91–98.

Spens, Janet. "A Study of Keats's 'Ode to a Nightingale.' " *The Review of English Studies*, n.s. 3 (1952): 234–43.

Sperry, Stuart M. *Keats the Poet*. Princeton: Princeton University Press, 1973.

Spiegelman, Willard. "Keats's 'Coming Muskrose' and Shakespeare's 'Profound Verdure.' " *Journal of English History* 50, no. 2 (1983): 347–62.

———. "The 'Ode to a Nightingale' and *Paradiso* XXIII." *Keats–Shelley Journal* 33 (1984): 37–40.

Spitzer, Leo. "The 'Ode on a Grecian Urn' or Content vs. Metagrammar." *Comparative Literature* 7 (1955): 203–25.

Stillinger, Jack, ed. *Twentieth Century Interpretations of Keats's Odes*. Englewood Cliffs, N.J.: Prentice-Hall, 1968.

Van Ghent, Dorothy. *Keats: The Myth of the Hero*. Princeton: Princeton University Press, 1983.

Vendler, Helen. *The Odes of John Keats*. Cambridge: Harvard University Press, 1983.

Waldoff, Leon. *Keats and the Silent Work of the Imagination*. Urbana: University of Illinois Press, 1985.

Wasserman, Earl R. *The Finer Tone: Keats's Major Poems*. Baltimore: The Johns Hopkins University Press, 1953.

Wentersdorf, Karl. "The Sub-Text of Keats's 'Ode to a Nightingale.' " *Keats–Shelley Journal* 33 (1984): 70–84.

# Acknowledgments

"Introduction" (originally entitled "John Keats") by Harold Bloom from *The Visionary Company* by Harold Bloom, © 1971 by Cornell University. Reprinted by permission of Cornell University Press.

"The 'Ode on Melancholy' " (originally entitled "The Odes of April and May, 1819") by Walter Jackson Bate from *John Keats* by Walter Jackson Bate, © 1963 by the President and Fellows of Harvard College. Reprinted by permission of The Belknap Press of Harvard University Press.

"The Fierce Dispute: The 'Ode to a Nightingale' " (originally entitled "The Fierce Dispute: The Odes") by Morris Dickstein from *Keats and His Poetry: A Study in Development* by Morris Dickstein, © 1971 by the University of Chicago. Reprinted by permission of the University of Chicago Press.

"In the Shadow of Milton: The 'Ode to Psyche' " (originally entitled "In the Shadow of Milton") by Harold Bloom from *A Map of Misreading* by Harold Bloom, © 1975 by Oxford University Press, Inc. Reprinted by permission of Oxford University Press, Inc.

"Poem and Ideology: A Study of Keats's 'To Autumn' " by Geoffrey H. Hartman from *Literary Theory and Structure,* edited by Frank Brady, John Palmer and Martin Price, © 1973 by Yale University. Reprinted by permission of Yale University Press. This essay was reprinted in *The Fate of Reading* (University of Chicago Press, 1975).

"Identification and Identity: The 'Ode to a Nightingale' " (originally entitled "Where the Daemon Is") by Stuart A. Ende from *Keats and the Sublime* by Stuart A. Ende, © 1976 by Yale University. Reprinted by permission of Yale University Press.

"Keats and a New Birth: The 'Ode on Melancholy' " (originally entitled "Keats and a New Birth") by Leslie Brisman from *Romantic Origins* by Leslie Brisman, © 1978 by Cornell University. Reprinted by permission of Cornell University Press.

143

"Voice in the Leaves: The 'Ode on a Grecian Urn' " (originally entitled "Voice in the Leaves: Three Odes of Keats") by Paul H. Fry from *The Poet's Calling in the English Ode* by Paul H. Fry, © 1980 by Yale University. Reprinted by permission of Yale University Press.

"The 'Ode on Indolence' " by Helen Vendler from *The Odes of John Keats* by Helen Vendler, © 1983 by the President and Fellows of Harvard College. Reprinted by permission of the Belknap Press of Harvard University Press.

"Silent Forms: The 'Ode to Psyche' and the 'Ode on a Grecian Urn' " by Martin Aske from *Keats and Hellenism: An Essay* by Martin Aske, © 1985 by Cambridge University Press. Reprinted by permission of Cambridge University Press.

# Index